THE WAR IN THE PENINSULA

SOME LETTERS OF A LANCASHIRE OFFICER

Memorial erected in Bolton Parish Church to
Lieutenant Robert Knowles.

THE WAR IN THE PENINSULA

SOME LETTERS

OF

LIEUTENANT ROBERT KNOWLES

Of the 7th, or Royal Fusiliers,
A Lancashire Officer

Arranged and Annotated by his Great-Great-Nephew
Sir Lees Knowles, Baronet,
CVO DL

The Spellmount Library of Military History

SPELLMOUNT
Staplehurst

British Library Cataloguing in Publication Data:
A catalogue record for this book is available
from the British Library

Copyright © Spellmount Ltd 2004
Introduction © Ian Fletcher 2004

ISBN 1-86227-235-2

First published in the UK in 1913 by
Tillotson & Son Ltd
Bolton

This edition first published in 2004
in
The Spellmount Library of Military History
by
Spellmount Limited
The Village Centre
Staplehurst
Kent TN12 0BJ

Tel: 01580 893730
Fax: 01580 893731
E-mail: enquiries@spellmount.com
Website: www.spellmount.com

1 3 5 7 9 8 6 4 2

Printed in Great Britain by
T.J. International Ltd, Padstow, Cornwall

AN INTRODUCTION
By Ian Fletcher

The British Army had been fighting in the Iberian Peninsula for almost a year when nineteen year-old Robert Knowles became a lieutenant in the Royal Lancashire Militia in July 1809. Born on 4 April 1790, Knowles joined the army at a time when Arthur Wellesley, commander-in-chief of the army in the Peninsula, was struggling to establish both himself and his army in Spain. After opening the campaign in August the previous year with two victories at Roliça and Vimeiro, Wellesley had been superseded by Sir Harry Burrard and Sir Hew Dalrymple who between them conspired to let the French off the hook, by allowing themselves to be drawn into a truce, the notorious Convention of Cintra. This particular arrangement allowed for the evacuation of all French troops in Portugal including those garrisoning the fortresses of Almeida and Elvas. It was the kind of agreement that would almost certainly – in part – be made today, as it freed Portugal from enemy troops without the loss of a single life. Otherwise, it is certain that hundreds would have become casualties on both sides had the British Army been forced to continue the fight both against the French field army, penned in by both the Tagus and the Atlantic, and against the strongly defended fortresses.

But if the British generals who signed the Convention thought it would prove to be an end to the French problem in Portugal they were sadly mistaken. True, it removed the invaders from the country but it caused a storm of protest and outrage in England. Enemy armies – especially those of Napoleon Bonaparte – were there to be thrashed and driven into the sea, not given a lift home to France, which is what both Dalrymple and Burrard – and, to an extent, Wellesley himself – agreed to. Furthermore, the French were given this ride home in the ships of the Royal Navy. And if this was not bad enough they were allowed to retain virtually all of their accumulated plunder along with their arms and most of their equipment. Little wonder that the popular saying of the day was, 'Oh, Cintral Britannia sickens at thy name.' The agreement which so outraged both the people and government in England was likewise criticised in Portugal, for although it had rid their country of the invaders, the negotiations had been conducted almost entirely without the input of the Portuguese authorities themselves who, one would imagine, would certainly have had their own ideas on how to treat the defeated enemy. The upshot was that Burrard and Dalrymple were recalled to face a Court of Inquiry, Wellesley having gone home on leave anyway. The British Army in the meantime fell under the command of Sir John Moore.

Moore's brave and well-intentioned but ultimately ill-fated Corunna campaign of 1808–09 not only resulted in his death at the Battle of Corunna, on 16 January 1809, but saw the British Army chased ignominiously from Spain by Marshal Soult, leaving around 10,000 British troops in Portugal under Sir John Craddock as our only presence in a country which was threatened once again by invading French forces. But all was not lost, for in April 1809 Sir Arthur Wellesley, acquitted of all charges arising from the Court of Inquiry, returned to command the British Army in Portugal and by the middle of the following month had swept the French from Portugal for a second time following his victory at Oporto on 12 May. Then, marching quickly southwards, he turned his attention to Marshal Victor, whose isolated force sat idly on the Tagus close to the Spanish town of Talavera where, on 27–28 July, Wellesley won a bloody and costly victory which won him the title of 'Wellington.'

Two days before the Battle of Talavera the new lieutenant in the Royal Lancashire Militia, Robert Knowles, was sitting in his quarters in Bristol, having travelled there by mail coach from Manchester. It was the start of two years with his regiment, during which he learned the basic rudiments of his profession, how to drill his men, the army system and, equally important, how to behave like a gentleman. Unfortunately, Knowles wrote no further letters – or if he did, they haven't survived – and thus all goes quiet for the next two years until May 1811, when Knowles joined the 7th (Royal) Fusiliers.

Robert Knowles' first letter home from his new quarters in Maidstone was written the month after his regiment had been involved in one of the bloodiest – if not the bloodiest – battle of the Peninsular War, Albuera. Fought on 16 May 1811, the battle saw numerous instances of individual and collective bravery, none more so than by Lieutenant Marthew Latham, of The Buffs, whose heroic defence of one of his regiment's colours cost him one of his arms and half of his face, and by Daniel Hoghton, who watched his brigade being cut to pieces around him, and yet still found time to change from his green coat into his regimental scarlet coat whilst still sitting in the saddle, and whilst enemy grape and musket shot flew all round him until he was struck down and killed. Regimental traditions were won at Albuera. It was here that the 57th (East) Middlesex Regiment won its nickname, 'The Die Hards,' for whilst the men of the regiment stood in an ever-dwindling line, torn apart by enemy fire at point-blank range, its commanding officer, William Inglis, himself struck down by a grape shot in the chest, lay behind them, refusing to be carried from the field and shouting, 'Die hard, 57th! Die hard!' And so they did. Inglis survived but of the 647 officers and men of his regiment who marched onto the field that morning, only 219 marched off of it.

But despite the tremendous and legendary fight put up by the men of Colborne's, Hoghton's and Abercrombie's brigades, the battle would almost certainly have been lost had it not been for the intervention of Lowry Cole and Henry Hardinge who, having seen the Allied commander, Marshal William Beresford, paralysed by indecision, took it upon themselves to launch the 4th Division – or at least Cole's Brigade – against the French in an attempt to wrest the initiative from the French. The ensuing advance remains one of the great moments in British military history as the Fusilier Brigade, consisting of two battalions of the 7th (Royal Fusiliers), and the 23rd (Royal Welsh) Fusiliers, supported by the Loyal Lusitanian Legion and the 11th and 23rd Portuguese, advanced into the maelstrom to turn the tide in the favour of the Allies. 'Nothing could stop that astonishing infantry,' wrote William Napier, the great historian of the war, and he was right. Nothing could, certainly not the French, and the Fusiliers stopped only after they stood bloodied and battered but triumphant on, 'that fatal hill.'

The news of the bloodbath at Albuera reached Maidstone just before 29 June 1811, for Knowles mentions it in a letter to his brother. Just how much of the gory details of the battle had been publicly circulated at this time is unknown. Certainly, it was too early for eye-witness accounts to have filtered through into the public domain. However, enough of the battle was known to have caused wild rumours to be circulated, for Knowles writes of a rumour claiming that Wellington (who was not even present at Albuera) had lost a leg, and that Beresford had been killed (given the British losses and the severity of the action, the blame for which can be squarely laid at Beresford's feet, there were some who would later claim that the death of Beresford would not have been a bad thing!). As Knowles' descendant writes, 'Rumour and false intelligence were very prevalent in those days.' They certainly were.

Robert Knowles can consider himself lucky he was not at

Albuera, otherwise he may well have been amongst the 706 casualties which the two battalions of the 7th suffered during the battle. Nevertheless, he was to see some bitter fighting himself during the two years he was in the Peninsula. He arrived in Lisbon in August 1811, at a time when, after a year of manoeuvring and countering, and after some hard fighting (in addition to Albuera, Wellington had just about overcome Marshal Massena at Fuentes de Oñoro on 3–5 May and had himself failed to take the fortress of Badajoz the following month) Wellington's army had settled down into positions on the Caia river to the south-west of Ciudad Rodrigo, the fortress that commanded the northern corridor between Spain and Portugal, waiting for an opportunity to attack.

During late September 1811, there were several clashes between Wellington and the French in front of Fuenteguinaldo, Wellington's headquarters, the most famous of which came on 25 September at El Bodon, where the cavalry of the King's German Legion, supported by British cavalry and infantry – in particular the 5th (Northumberland) Fusiliers – performed heroics against a vastly superior French cavalry force. Knowles himself saw action two days later, at Aldea da Ponte, his first smell of powder in the Peninsula.

By the end of the year Wellington had moved further north as he turned his attention towards Ciudad Rodrigo. Four companies of the 7th Fusiliers, including Knowles, were despatched to the north of the fortress, to the small village of Barba del Puerco, which overlooks the river Agueda and the only bridge over the river north of Ciudad Rodrigo. One can almost see him and his comrades, standing on the vast, flat rocks, gazing down into the immense gorge at the great Roman bridge that spans the roaring waters of the Agueda. On 19 January 1812 Ciudad Rodrigo was stormed by the 3rd and Light Divisions. Knowles himself worked hard in the miserable, cold trenches before the town, undertaking

24-hour shifts, but he was disappointed when his division was relieved by the 3rd Division on 19 January for it meant that he was denied the opportunity of taking part in the storming.

Knowles was not to wait for too long before he had another chance to take part in a storming, for barely two months after the capture of Ciudad Rodrigo, Wellington's men were back in the south, and were positioned in front of the tremendously strong walls of the fortress of Badajoz, which commanded the southern corridor between Spain and Portugal. The fortress had denied Wellington in June 1811 and, indeed, ever since 1809 when British troops wounded at Talavera were left in the town, only to be poorly cared for by the people – known to be pro-French – the place had attracted a very bad reputation amongst Wellington's men. Their feelings were amply summed up by Lieutenant William Grattan, soon to be wounded during the storming, who wrote, 'In a word, the capture of Badajoz had long been their [the British] idol; many causes led to this wish on their part; the two previous unsuccessful sieges, and the failure of the attack against San Christobal in the latter; but above all, the well-known hostility of its inhabitants to the British army, and, perhaps might be added, a desire for plunder which the sacking of Rodrigo had given them a taste for. Badajoz was, therefore, denounced as a place to be made example of; and unquestionably no city, Jerusalem exempted, was ever more strictly visited to the letter than was this ill-fated town.'

And so it was, for on the momentous night of 6 April 1812 the fortress of Badajoz was assaulted by the full force of Wellington's army. Attacks were made on the three breaches made in the walls, whilst two other attacks were made by escalade at the castle and on the San Vicente bastion. Knowles himself was fortunate that he was spared the horror of the assaults on the breaches, for his regiment was ordered to attack the Fort San Roque, 200 yards or so outside the walls of the town. It was here that the French had constructed a dam which caused the forming of an inundation or false lake in front of the breaches, something which caused the stormers so many problems. In the event, Knowles was lucky to escape with nothing more than a badly wounded hand when a piece of grape shot dashed his sword into pieces. 'I providentially escaped without any serious injury, although my clothes were torn from my back,' he wrote, adding, 'My sword hand is much cut and bruised, which accounts for my bad writing, and my right side is a little bruised.'

Wellington's infantry made over forty separate attacks on the breaches, and forty times they were driven back by a very tenacious garrison commanded by Baron Armand Phillipon. His efforts were ultimately in vain, however, for the two attacks by escalade, intended to be simply diversionary attacks, succeeded and the town was won at last. But at what a cost! Nearly 3,500 men were killed or wounded during the storming, and these concentrated into two small areas in front of the breaches and at the foot of the castle walls. Little wonder, therefore, that Wellington broke down and wept when he saw the devastation at the breaches on the morning of 7 April. By then, of course, Wellington's vengeful troops, driven to the point of madness by the fury of their assaults, were well and truly engaged on an orgy of pillage, murder, drunkenness and destruction. And well earned it was too, they would say, for the French had defied convention and had refused to surrender even though practical breaches had been made in the walls of the town. Seventy-two hours later, the disorder, 'subsided, rather than was quelled,' and the dazed and exhausted British troops staggered away, laden with plunder and with mightily-sore heads, but triumphant, having presented Wellington with the second of the 'keys to Spain.'

A threat by Marshal Marmont to Ciudad Rodrigo caused

Wellington to return north, rather than head east along the valley of the Tagus towards Madrid, the logical route. The threat was averted and, in June 1812, Wellington was on the march northeast towards Salamanca, the beautiful university town, and a great base for the French armies in central Spain. After weeks of manoeuvring the two armies finally fell in with each other and by the afternoon of 22 July were face to face looking out across the great, dusty plain to the south of the small village of Los Arapile. Unfortunately for the French, a combination of a lapse in concentration and overconfidence, led to their army becoming over-extended, something which Wellington was quick to seize upon. By the end of the day the Allies had completely smashed Marmont's army, and it was only the unauthorised withdrawal by Carlos d'Espana of Spanish troops guarding the bridge over the River Tormes at Alba de Tormes, which allowed the French to make good their escape and take the shine off what was otherwise a crushing victory for Wellington.

Salamanca also saw Robert Knowles receive his second wound of the war. And a far more serious one it might have been if the musket ball which struck him in the arm had hit home with more force than it did. 'I had it cut out the same night,' he wrote, 'and I believe the bone is not injured.' Knowles was lucky, for in 1812 the usual course for surgeons presented with broken bones resulting from gunshot wounds was to reach for the amputating saw. Despite playing down his wound, Knowles was listed as severely wounded, whilst he also suffered from 'fever and ague' as well as what he called, 'a most severe bowel complaint' He also complained – as did most of Wellington's officers – of a lack of funds, the army being almost permanently in a state of arrears of pay. Indeed, it was a sorry thing for an officer to be without money whilst on campaign and Knowles is certainly not alone in writing home about the problem.

1812 ended in massive frustration and disappointment for Wellington. Despite all of the triumphs – Ciudad Rodrigo, Badajoz, Salamanca and the occupation of Madrid – he ended the year where he began; back in Portugal. After his army had marched into Madrid on 12 August he took himself off to lay siege to Burgos, a siege that went disastrously wrong from the outset. With too few troops, and even fewer heavy guns, the siege staggered on through September and October until by the 22nd of that month, with French forces gathering to the north, Wellington was forced into an ignominious withdrawal. The weather turned against him, the commissariat broke down, the discipline of many of the troops dissolved and the whole episode turned into a repeat – some say worse – of the retreat to Corunna.

Knowles was spared the rigours of the retreat owing to his detachment to the regimental depot at Santarem, on the Tagus, north of Lisbon. Unfortunately, there is only a single letter from here, in which Knowles at least had the satisfaction of enjoying an increase in pay owing to a staff appointment. The letter to his Father, written in February 1813, is, sadly, the last. By the spring of 1813 Wellington had crossed the border into Spain once again, embarking upon his final – and decisive – campaign. On 21 June he crushed the French at Vittoria, a victory which effectively spelled the end of French ambitions in the Peninsula. The victory opened up the way for an invasion of France itself and the following month Wellington had driven the French back over the Pyrenees. But the French were not giving up without a fight. Indeed, on 25 July they launched an offensive against the passes at Maya and Roncesvalles in an attempt to drive through to the beleaguered French garrison of Pamplona. It was during this fighting – the battles between 25 July and 2 August subsequently became known as the Battle of the Pyrenees – that Robert Knowles was killed.

The pass of Roncesvalles, once held centuries before by the immortal Roland against the Basque hordes, is marked by two massive hills to the east and west. The French attacks to the east were held back for around four hours by a few hundred light infantrymen ensconced in some rocks before the pressure told and they were pulled back. On the western side of the pass, on the Linduz Plateau, General Ross – soon to fall at Bladensburg – led his brigade up to face the French under General Reille. It was a fierce fight, Major Tovey's company of the 20th Regiment getting stuck into the enemy with their bayonets, with Tovey himself crying, 'Bayonet away! Bayonet away!' Into the fray were thrust the 7th Fusiliers, Knowles amongst them. We are not sure how he died, but somewhere up on that narrow path, overlooking the magnificent scenery of both France and Spain, Knowles met his death, the only officer of the Fusiliers to be killed during the battle.

Robert Knowles still lies somewhere up on the Linduz Plateau today. The British troops were driven off by Reille's men who would – hopefully – have buried Knowles, along with their own casualties. There was certainly no chance for the British to undertake the task. If he wasn't buried by the French, it would have been a good few days before the British returned. At Maya, fought on the same day as Roncesvalles, the British dead lay exposed both to the elements and to wild animals and were interred by their comrades when they returned a week or two after the fight

Knowles was no different from hundreds of other British officers who died in the line of fire whilst on active service in the Peninsula. Ralph Bunbury, of the 95th was the first, killed at Obidos on 15 August 1808, The last died at Bayonne on 14 April 1814. It is fortunate, however, that his memory lives on, not only in the memorial in his church at St Peter, Bolton-le-Moore, in Lancashire, but in these letters, reprinted for the first time since 1913, and the latest worthy title in the library of Spellmount Classics.

THE WAR IN THE PENINSULA

———➤●●◄———

SOME LETTERS

OF

Lieutenant ROBERT KNOWLES,

Of the 7th, or Royal, Fusiliers,
A Lancashire Officer.

————

Arranged and Annotated by his Great-Great-Nephew

SIR LEES KNOWLES, BARONET,

C.V.O., D.L.

—————

JULY 25th, 1913.

Printed and Published by Tillotson & Son, Lt?.,
Mealhouse Lane, Bolton.
1913.

PREFACE.

The following lines are from a letter, dated June 28th, 1913, written by Professor C. W. C. Oman, M.A., of All Souls College, Professor of Modern History (Chichele) in Oxford University :—

" I rejoice to see that there is to be a second edition of these interesting letters, which contain not only a record of the daily life of the 4th Division, with all the details of its toils and marches, but several pieces of narrative of real historical value, especially with regard to the fights at Albuera, Aldea da Ponte, and Salamanca. The writer was a keen and intelligent young soldier, and his letters have not only a special interest for those who are connected with the old 7th, the Royal Fusiliers, but also much that all who care to know about the British Army in the Penin--sula will be glad to read."

The War in the Peninsula

INTRODUCTION.

THESE letters were written a hundred years ago by my great-great-uncle, Lieutenant Robert Knowles, and I believe that they, and the notes of Sergeant John Spencer Cooper, are the only contemporary regimental record of the 7th, or Royal, Fusiliers. They came into the possession of his niece, Margaret Mary Knowles, a daughter of James Knowles, who was Town Clerk of Bolton. They were lent years ago to my father, and he made a copy of them. In 1890, I compared the copy with the originals, which were in a fragile state—moreover, some of them were missing —and this reproduction is from a copy which I made at the time of the comparison. Some of the original letters are again before me. The handwriting shows con--siderable care, and it is very different from what one would expect in letters written during a campaign. The letters are printed here in their entirety, and the original spelling has been retained. Each letter is folded twice, in long strips, the creases being at right angles to the writing, and the ends of the strips folded together, and sealed in the middle as a rule with red sealing-wax, in several instances bearing, from the impress of a military button, a rose with the legend round it, *Honi soit qui mal y pense.* The address is lengthwise on the back of the sheet. On the letter of July 7th, 1811, is printed in red, square, straight letters, " Maidstone." On the letter of August 29th, 1811, is the circular postmark, "Portsmouth, 1 Oc. 1. 1811. 73."; on the letter of Nov. 5th, 1811, is the postmark, " Lisbon, De. 13. 1811. F." ; on the letter of Dec. 31st, 1811, is the postmark, " Lisbon, Ja. 22. 1812 "; on the letter of Jan. 20th, 1812, is the postmark, " Lisbon, Feb. 18. 1812 " ; and, on the letter of Sept. 23rd, 1812, is the postmark, " Lisbon, Se. 23. 1812." On several letters, printed in black, is the expression " Packet Letter," with a town after it, such as " Plymouth," and several of them have " 2/5 " written upon the face of them. The letter of the Duke of Wellington bears the old blue twopenny stamp, and it is sealed with his crest surrounded by the garter and surmounted by a coronet.

The first of the six volumes of the History of the War in the Peninsula and in the South of France, from the year 1807 to the year 1814, by Major-General Sir William F. P. Napier, K.C.B., Colonel 27th Regiment, contains the story of the first portion of the war ending in May, 1809, just two months earlier than the first of the letters hereafter printed. That History, full of glowing language and brilliant description, and the admirable, carefully-balanced, and probably more accurate History of the War by Professor

Oman, contain all that is essential in connection with this glorious epoch of British military history. The treaty of Tilsit had given Napoleon a commanding position in Europe, and had brought him directly into conflict with England. France and England were both strong, but the battle of Trafalgar had prevented the invasion of England, and Napoleon therefore proposed to weaken her naval and commercial strength by barring the Con--tinent against English manufactures. It was necessary to do this by French troops. Portugal was virtually an unguarded province of England, whence, and from Gibraltar, English goods passed into Spain. To check this traffic by force was not easy. Spain was to France nearly what Portugal was to England, and the French cause was therefore popular in Spain, and the weak Court of Spain was subservient. Napoleon, accordingly, proposed to place his brother, Joseph Bonaparte, then King of Naples, upon the Spanish Throne, and eventually on July 24th, 1808, he was proclaimed King of Spain and the Indies, becoming, however, the object of a nation's hatred. The volume deals with the principal operations in the Eastern and Central Provinces, and, having shown that the Spaniards, however restless, were unable to throw off the yoke, the writer turns to Portugal, where the invasion was first stayed, and finally forced back by greater strength.

L. K.

JULY 25TH, 1913.

THE WAR IN THE PENINSULA

AND

THE STORY OF A LANCASHIRE OFFICER.

———————

OLD letters, more than old books bring us into direct contact with men of a past age. As we read their exact words and see their hand-writing we seem to know them, and they become real living beings and not figures of imagination, however powerfully portrayed. With soldiers, taking into consideration men of action in every sphere of public life, this is perhaps more true than with any other class, as their work in the world is necessarily more arresting, more striking, more immediately effective.

In these letters, we have an account of stirring events, written within a few days of their occurrence by a young Officer who had himself taken part in them. He gives his experiences and impressions modestly, and like most British Officers, he is under, rather than over the mark, in stating their value where his own deeds are concerned. When he tells his father that his wounds are slight, the despatches say " severe." His description of the sufferings of the sick and wounded after Salamanca is not as painful reading as those of the historians who have examined every particle of evidence. The statements made in these letters bear the test of comparison with the official reports, contemporary letters and narratives. As we read, we feel that we are in touch with a man of knowledge, and a soldier, whose patriotism took him into the battle--field. He had not the inducement of monetary reward ; for, after the manner of his kind, he had to pay, and pay heavily, to serve his country.

Such an example should not be forgotten, or the memory of heroism and of self-sacrifice be buried in oblivion. For a well-informed, patriotic, nation, time brightens rather than dims the lustre of the fame of soldiers who have fallen in battle, and the glories of the War in the Peninsula have been revived by the series of centenaries that have been celebrated since 1908. A nation or country forgetful of its past history is one that is doomed to defeat and decay.

1 8 0 9 .

The year 1809 opened badly for England. An illus--trious soldier was struck down in the very moment of his victory. Sir John Moore had led the Army committed to his care with consummate skill. His retreat on Corunna accomplished its purpose, and justified his foresight. The Emperor Napoleon at the head of his hitherto victorious legions was drawn from Madrid, whither fate decreed that he was never to return. The soldiers who fought under Moore returned to England worn out by privation and hardships. Within a few months they were again hastened to South Beveland on what was known as the Walcheren Expedition, and then, without accomplishing any useful purpose, they returned to England decimated by fever, many dying, and a large proportion of the survivors remain--ing for some years in a state of convalescence. Ireland at that time absorbed an Army of no less than 60,000 men. England was garrisoned largely by the constitutional force, the Militia. One regiment, the Royal Lancaster, was embodied and quartered at Bristol, and the writer of these letters joined it there in July, 1809.

Robert Knowles was the fourth son of Robert Knowles, of Quarlton and Eagley Bank, Little Bolton, in the County of Lancaster. He was born on April 4th, 1790, and in 1809 he was gazetted as Lieutenant in the Royal Lan--caster Regiment.

The first letter to his father gives a glimpse of the old coaching-days, a journey of thirteen hours from Man--chester to Birmingham, a crowded Mail-coach necessitating the delay of one night, and then an all-day journey to Bristol. The letter is dated Bristol, July 25th, 1809, and the reader will notice the coincidence that the day was a fatal one for the writer.

To Mr. Robert Knowles.

Bristol, July 25th, 1809.

Dear Father,—I now sit down to inform you of my safe arrival at Bristol. I left Manchester at half-past one o'clock on Saturday morning, accompanied by Lieut. Bottomley, and we arrived at Birmingham at half-past two o'clock Saturday evening, from which town the mail was filled, so that we were obliged to stop one night at Birmingham. We immediately took seats in the stage--coach, which sets off early on Sunday morning, and arrived at this place at nine o'clock on Sunday evening. We had a very pleasant and agreeable journey. On Monday morning we waited upon the Colonel, and I delivered Capt. Mason's letter to his friend, Lieut. Bythesea, by whom I have been very handsomely received. He intro--duced me to the officers of the Regiment, who appear to be very agreeable gentlemen. Lieut. Bythesea's best respects to Capt. Mason, and please to inform him that he has a little boy. Please to return Capt. Mason my sincere thanks for the kindness shown unto me. Mr. Bottomley and myself have taken lodgings in College Place, which consists of two bedrooms and one parlour, for which we are to pay 21s. per week. Bristol is a very large and pleasant city, and the docks are full of shipping in consequence of the embargo. We have very bad news from abroad, but hope it will be better than what is re--presented. On Monday night there was a fatal duel in the French prison near this place between two of the prisoners. The weapons they fought with were two pieces of broken files, about six inches long, sharpened and tyed at the end of sticks. They fought a considerable time, when one of them was stuck to the heart. If you do see *Mr. Orrell desire him to join as soon as possible, as I think it would be much better for him, as he will have more to learn than he is aware of.

I will write again in the course of a week. I am very anxious to hear how my †Grandfather is, and I do hope this will find you and all the family in good health. Please to remember me to all enquiring friends. With the greatest affection and respect for you, my brothers, sisters, and all relations.—I subscribe myself,

Your affectionate Son,

R. Knowles.

P.S.—I hope you will not delay writing to me. Please to address—

> Lieut. Knowles,
> > 1st R.L. Militia,
> > > Bristol.

In haste and a bad pen.

---

* Lieutenant Andrew Orrell.

† Andrew Knowles, of Quarlton, and of Eagley Bank, Little Bolton, the only surviving son of Robert Knowles : buried at Turton, Feb. 8, 1810, aged 74 : will dated Oct. 11, 1809, proved at Chester, August 25, 1810.

There is here a long break of two years in the letters which have been preserved. The next is a short note from Hull, written on May 25th, 1811, when the writer was in daily expectation of receiving a commission in the regular army.

To Mr. Robert Knowles.

Hull, 25th May, 1811.

Dear Father,—As I gave you reason to expect me at home about this time, I think it my duty to inform you that I cannot leave the Regiment until my name appears in the Gazette, which I hope will be in a few days, after which I will lose no time in repairing home. We have no news here worth committing to paper, particularly as I am very soon expecting to see you. Please to remember me to my sisters, brothers, and all enquiring friends.

Your affectionate Son.

(Name torn off.)

THE 7TH ROYAL FUSILIERS.

On May 7th, 1811, Robert Knowles was appointed Lieutenant in the 7th Royal Fusiliers, then, as now, one of the most distinguished regiments in the Army ; and, within a month, he was at Maidstone where he had joined the Depôt of his Regiment.

This letter tells the home-circle of his arrival, and gives some information about the uniform and expenses of those days. Six guineas for the stamp on a first commission was a heavy tax for a young officer. As is not even now-a-days unusual, the tailor came in for the chief share of the spoil, with a bill of £20 for a regimental coat and wings.

To Mr. Robert Knowles.

Maidstone, 23rd June, 1811.

Dear Father,—I arrived at London about ten o'clock on the evening of the 19th, and at Maidstone on the evening of the 21st, where I was well received by the commanding officer and officers of the Regiment at present with the Depôt. There is a draft of four hundred men and nine officers (including myself) ordered to be in readiness to proceed to Portsmouth to embark for Portugal on the 25th inst., but we have not yet received our route, and I think it probable it will be put off a few days longer. I wish you to send me by the Defiance Coach from the Bridgewater Arms, Manchester, which leaves at four o'clock in the evening, my large box (if it is yet arrived from Hull), with my two old regimental coats, white pantaloons, two pair blue pantaloons, the best I have got, two sashes, sword knot, cocked hat, shoes, pair of boots, linen, bed-linen, two black silk handkerchiefs, paper-case, and any other things that I have got which you think will be of use to me. I am very sorry I did not see my brother *Chadwick at Manchester, and it hurt me much to leave my sister alone, but I hope she very soon found him. When we receive our route I will write you by that day's post. We are seven days' march from Portsmouth. I am going to London to-morrow to stop a few days, where I

* Third son of Robert Knowles, of Eagley Bank, Little Bolton : born Jan. 27th, and baptized at Bolton, Feb. 24th, 1786 : died, un--married, Dec. 17th, 1817 : buried at Turton.

B

intend providing myself with everything that is necessary.
I am under the necessity of requesting you will send me
£30 by return of post (underneath you have an estimate of
my expenses), which I hope will be the last sum I shall
trouble you for until my return from abroad. Please to
remember me to my brothers, sisters, and all enquiring
friends.

Your affectionate Son,

R. Knowles, Lt., Royal Fusiliers.

Estimate of my Expense :—	£	s.	d.
Regimental Coat and Wings	20	0	0
Sabre	4	4	0
Cap	6	6	0
Large Blue Pantaloons and Chain	2	5	0
Three Pair Shoes and Gaiters	2	14	0
Belt and Breast Plate	2	0	0
Commission	6	6	0
Plate			
Sundrys			
	£43	**15**	**0**

The above is the lowest estimate, and I am having my
old coat cut down for a service jacket, which will be an
expense of three or four pounds in gold lace, &c.

My address in London, where I shall remain until
Saturday next :—

Lieut. Knowles, 7th Royal Fusiliers,

No. 28, Suffolk Street,

Charing Cross, London.

Directions for my large box :—

Lt. Knowles, 7th Royal Fusiliers, Maidstone,

to be forwarded by the coach from the Golden Cross,
Charing Cross, London.

P.S.—If you can send my box by the Defiance Coach on Thursday I shall receive it at London. In that case, direct it to be left at the Coach Office till called for. Please mention the direction in your letter, which I hope you will not fail to send by return of post.

I intended writing yesterday, but there was no post from this town with speed.

P.S.—I have this moment received a parcel from home, also a letter from my brother. Therefore, it will be unnecessary sending me bed-linen or anything else, unless I find it necessary to write for them when I get to Ports--mouth, but I hope you will not fail sending me the sum I have wrote for by return of post, after seeing Capt. Robinson's letter.

Lieutenant Knowles was in London on June 29th, 1811, and the victory to which he refers in his letter of that date must have been the Battle of Albuera, fought on May 16th. Marshal Beresford, and not Wellington, com--manded the Allies.

Rumour and false intelligence were very prevalent in those days. The distance, the difficulties of communication, the uncertainty of sailing-ships, the stories circulated by interested parties, both friends and foes, all tended to create fiction, sometimes alarming, and often harassing.

To Mr. Chadwick Knowles.

London, June 29th, 1811.

Dear Brother,—I have just received yours of the 27th instant, enclosing a £30 draft and one pound note, for which

I return my Father my sincere thanks. You have given me Mr. John Woods' address, but it was unnecessary, having called upon him twice, but have nothing to thank him for but mere civility. We have no further information res--pecting our march, but expect it daily. You mention my sister's letter that she wrote me. I shall take an opportunity of answering it in a few days. I intend re--turning to Maidstone on Monday next. I should have deferred writing until to-morrow, having received your letter so late in the evening, but for a report there is in Town that there has been a very severe action in Spain, in which our army was crowned with victory, but with very severe loss. Report says that Lord Wellington has lost a leg, and that Marshall Beresford is killed, but the French army is entirely dispersed. It is believed by many people in the Town, but I am very doubtful, as it is a French account, and it is unusual for them to spread reports to their dis--advantage. I have not time to write anything more unless I lose the advantage of to-night's post.

Please to remember me to all our family and enquiring friends, and believe me,

Your affectionate Brother,

R. Knowles, Lt., Royal Fusiliers.

Excuse haste and a bad pen.

To his sister are given particulars of the final marching orders, and the keen spirit of the soldier is shown in his desire to take his place in the field against the enemies of his country.

Note.—This letter is sealed with red sealing-wax, bearing the impress of a button, on which is a central heraldic rose with the in--scription round it of *"Honi soit qui mal y pense"*, partly legible.

To Miss Knowles.

Maidstone, July 7th, 1811.

My dear Sister,—I received yours of the 20th ult. in due time, and am glad to see you give yourself credit for not opening my letters, but I still think that a female's curiosity will not be satisfied until she knows the contents. You say that you have heard a report that the officers of our Regiment are returning from Spain, but I am happy to inform you that there is not the least foundation for the report. So far from it that we nine officers and 400 men have received our route to march for Portsmouth on Wednesday and Thursday next, there to embark to join our gallant comrades in Spain. I am ordered to march with the 2nd Division on Thursday, and shall arrive at Portsmouth on Wednesday, the 17th instant, where I expect to hear from home on my arrival with a parcel containing the remainder of my shirts, night--shirts, stockings, bed-linen, military books, French books, brace of small pistols with the moulds, and portmanteaus. I am induced to write for those things, our Regiment having a store at Lisbon, where I intend leaving most of my baggage, as I can at any time send for everything that is necessary to that place. I spent my time very pleasantly in London, where I remained about eight days. I was in a private lodging-house along with an officer of our Regiment, who knows a great deal of the town, and he was so obliging as to go with me wherever I pleased. I wish you to forward the parcel by the coach on the 12th or 13th, with directions to be left till called for. Before I take leave of Old England I will write to my father, and every future opportunity that occurs I shall take great pleasure in writing to my friends in Lancashire. I shall endeavour to see Lieut. Woods in Spain ; if his friends have anything to send to him I should be happy to take charge of it. Please to remember me to my father, brothers, sisters, and all enquiring friends, and believe me,

Your affectionate Brother,

Robt. Knowles, Lt.,

Royal Fusiliers.

P.S.—It is dinner-hour, therefore must conclude.*

A march of seven days brought Lieutenant Knowles and the detachment of the 7th Royal Fusiliers from Maid--stone to Hilsea Barracks, Portsmouth, on July 17th, 1811. The embarkation took place on the following day. Adverse winds detained the fleet of transports for a week at Spit--head, where the following letter was written on July 24th, 1811 :—

To Mr. Robert Knowles.

Spithead, July 24th, 1811.

My dear Father,—I take the latest opportunity of addressing you on leaving for a short time my much--beloved country. I must commence with our march from Maidstone to Portsmouth, which was a very pleasant one. We passed through Tunbridge, Tunbridge Wells, East Grinstead, Horsham, Petworth, Chichester to Hilsea Barracks, near Portsmouth, where we arrived on the 17th, and embarked early on the morning of the 18th, in the Matilda Transport No. 68. We immediately dropped down to Spithead, where we have since remained, weather bound, but there is now a fair wind, and we expect to sail

---

*This letter is also sealed.

in the course of the day. I have received a trunk from home. Inclosed I found a kind letter from you. My brother's letter is also come to hand, in which he informs me that I might expect to see Mr. Orrel (*sic*) in Portsmouth. He is arrived and on board the Arethusa transport, but I have not yet seen him. I went on board that vessel yesterday, but he was on shore. If possible I will see him in the course of the day, as my brother informs me he has a portmanteau in charge for me. There is a large fleet of transports going to Portugal from this place, with about three thousand troops on board. If we have a quick passage we shall be a very seasonable supply for Lord Wellington. Our detach--ment is about 370 strong, in high spirits, and anxious to join their brave comrades in Spain. 27th.—The wind is now fair, and the fleet is now getting under weigh. We have no news, therefore must conclude. Trusting I shall have the pleasure of seeing my dear father, brothers, and sisters all in good health on my return,

> I remain, dear Father,
> Your affectionate Son,
> R. Knowles, Lt.,
> Royal Fusiliers.

In haste.

P.S.—I have seen Mr. Orrel ; he is in good health. I forgot to say that the wind changed on the 24th, therefore delayed finishing my letter for a few days. You shall hear from me on my arrival at Lisbon.

The Fleet was compelled to put into Falmouth, and the last letter he was fated to write within sight of his native land was written from the Cornish port. It is easy to imagine the impatience of 10 Officers and 370 men,

" cabined, cribbed, confined," for sixteen days in a sailing transport, between Spithead and Falmouth, with little comfort and indifferent food. Biscuit and salt beef was then the staple ration of our soldiers, and even that was not always in a sound and wholesome condition. In those days such meat, supplied for long voyages, was called " junk," because it resembled old rope-ends in hardness and toughness. But, there was in some measure compensation in a quick trip to Lisbon, as twelve days was good sailing in the early years of the Nineteenth Century.

To Mr. Robert Knowles.

Falmouth Harbour, Aug. 9th, 1811,
on board Matilda Transport.

Dear Father,—You will see in the public prints an account of our arrival at this place. We were obliged to put in by contrary winds on the morning of the 2nd inst. I have delayed writing, expecting hourly to set sail, when I hope we shall be more fortunate. The fleet for Lisbon consists of about seventy sail. We are on board the fastest sailer and the finest transport in the fleet. Contrary to my expectation I have not experienced the least sea-sickness, and I am happy to say our men continue in the best state of health. You will see in this month's Army list how fortunate I am in my appointment, as there are now eight lieuts. junior to me. I saw Mr. Orrel in Falmouth on Wednesday last. He told me that he had wrote home and mentioned that he had seen me. The last accounts from our Regiment, the 2nd Battalion were under orders for England, but I hope the orders will be countermanded. On my arrival in Portugal, I hope I shall have the pleasure of receiving a letter from you. Please to remember me to my brothers, sisters, and all enquiring friends, and believe me,

Your affectionate Son,

R. Knowles, Lt.,

Royal Fusiliers.

P.S.—We are now under sail. Adieu ! Please to direct : Lt. Knowles, 7th Royal Fusiliers, with the Army in Portugal.

Two letters from Portugal describe the impression which Lisbon, the capital, made on the soldiers, upon their arrival there.

To Mr. Robert Knowles.

Lisbon, August 24th, 1811.

Dear Father,—I am happy to inform you of my arrival at this place on the 21st inst. We had a very good passage from Falmouth, and landed at Lisbon on the 22nd inst. Our men are quartered in the Convent of Carmo, but we expect daily to march to the Army. Our detachment was very fortunate in leaving England before the arrival of our 2nd Battalion, which has left Lisbon about three weeks. I was very sorry to see so many of our brave fellows sick and wounded in the hospitals at Lisbon and Belem. A great many of our officers are at Lisbon sick and wounded, many of them without hopes of recovery. A Lieut. Jones, of our Regiment, died yesterday. The last accounts from our Army they were blockading Ciudad Rodrigo—our

Regiment is attached to the Light Division. To give you a description of Lisbon—the town is well built, and stands on the rise of a hill, but the streets smell abominably. The filthy inhabitants throw their dirt into the streets as soon as it is dark, and they pay little attention to clearing it away in the morning. I will return the letters for Lieut. Woods and Richard Booth, of the 48th Regiment, the first opportunity, understanding they have left this country for England. I will write to you as soon as we join the Regiment. I am informed that we are to march through the most barren country, laid waste by the army. We have no news here, and have not heard from England since our arrival. Be so good as to remember me to all enquiring friends, particularly to my dear sisters and brothers, and believe me,

Your affectionate Son,

R. Knowles, Lt.,

Royal Fusiliers.

P.S.—I am sorry I have delayed writing until half an hour before the sailing of the Packet, but lost no time in writing after receiving the information, therefore you must excuse all mistakes and the shortness of the letter. We are about 250 miles from the Army.

To Mr. Robert Knowles.

Lisbon, 29th August, 1811.

Dear Father,—I avail myself of this opportunity of forwarding the enclosed letters to Mr. Wood, understanding that both his son and Richard Booth are returned to England with the 2nd Battalion of the 48th. We embark to-morrow morning to sail up the Mondego as far as Coim--bra, so that we shall be a few days at sea. I mentioned to

you in my last letter that Lisbon is a dirty town ; it is also
infested with a multitude of dogs, which no person owns.
On account of their infernal howling (all the night) I
could not sleep for several nights after my arrival. I
wrote in my last that our men were quartered in the Con-
-vent of Carmo. The officers are all billeted in private
houses. We have our regular rations of beef and biscuits,
but the meat we have is so poor that it would be burnt
if exposed for sale in Bolton Market. At present we are
in a town where there is plenty of good things. When we
leave, John Bull must give up his idea of good living. I
have not seen Mr. Orrel since my arrival in Lisbon, but hear
that he marches in a few days to join his Regiment, which
is with General Hill's Division near Badajos. I am appre-
-hensive that the officers of this detachment, after our arrival
at the Army, will be ordered back to England to join our
2nd Battalion, which is to be quartered in Yorkshire,
either at York, Beverley, or Richmond. Yesterday a very
fine vessel was burnt in the Tagus. She had been used
as a store ship. Our regimental stores were taken out of
her a few days ago, but I hear the heavy baggage of three
other regiments is entirely destroyed. The last accounts
from the Army, our Light troops were advancing, and the
3rd Division had invested Ciudad Rodrigo. The weather
is very hot, but I hope our marches to join the Army will
be made in the night as much as possible. I am daily
expecting to hear from home, and hope you will often write
and give me all the news you can. Give my love to my
brothers and sisters, and remember me to all enquiring
friends. Your affectionate Son,

R. Knowles, Lt., Royal Fusiliers.

I send this per favour of Mr. Pennie, of our Regiment,
who returns to England in consequence of severe wounds.
Postmark, " Portsmouth, 1 Oc. 1, 1811."

THE CAMPAIGN IN THE PENINSULA.

After a delay of one week at Lisbon, the detachments started to join the Army under Lord Wellington. The party of the 7th Royal Fusiliers, in strength nearly equal to half a battalion, was commanded by Lieutenant Charles Barrington, a young officer of three years' service. This is an illustration of the youth of the soldiers who were sent to fill the depleted ranks of Wellington's Army. Another Officer, Lieutenant Cameron, who was serving with this draft records in his Journal that " the men were so young, and were worked so hard, that before the winter was over, 300 had either died or been sent home to England". The following letter gives the line of march, and, considering the times, and that it was written in a cantonment without any facilities for writing, it is a remarkably good letter.

Aldea de Bisboa, Oct. 7th, 1811.

Dear Father,— I have now the satisfaction of addressing you from a Spanish town, after a long and fatiguing march through Portugal. I wrote you last when on the point of sailing for the river Mondego, where we anchored after three days' passage on the 4th Sept., and immediately landed at Figueras. On the 8th, we commenced our march for the Army. We passed through Monte Mor and Perona to Coimbra, where we arrived on the 11th. On the 14th we proceeded on our march through Algacia, Moita, Galleces, Meneca, Sampayo, Celonio, Bacasal, Castell Boni, Navo de Vene to Fuentes de Quinaldo (the headquarters of Lord Wellington and also of General Cole, who commands the 4th Division of the Army), where we arrived on the morning of the 25th. At the time our advanced brigade was engaged with the enemy. The Fusilier Brigade had marched about half an hour when we arrived to cover the retreat of the advance, the particulars of which you will see in the Gazette. Our Regiment advanced in line with the 23rd and 48th in close column on each flank, when, having accomplished their object, they gradually returned to their position, where we had the pleasure of joining them.

Robert Knowles reached Fuente Guinaldo on September 25th, 1811, and it may perhaps be of assistance to the reader if an outline be given of the position of the Army in Portugal, and of the 7th Royal Fusiliers at this time.

On May 16th, 1811, the battle of Albuera was won by the British soldier, and not by the General-ship of the Com--manders of the allied troops engaged. The hill of Albuera is celebrated in military histories. Imagine six thousand British soldiers fighting for four hours against heavy odds to gain its crest, a heavy rain falling and sometimes obscuring the enemy from their view, and the water-courses of the hill-side coloured with blood ! Of the six thousand, only fifteen hundred reached the crest of the hill unwounded. A memorable example of British endurance and pluck.

The 7th Royal Fusiliers and the 23rd Fusiliers formed the Fusilier Brigade of the 4th Division, and in a crisis of the battle these soldiers, under the leader-ship of Lt.-Colonel

Sir William Myers of the 7th, forced their way up the hill, struck and shattered a division of the French in flank, and recaptured six guns. Of those who fought at Albuera it would be invidious to select any Regiment, or section ; but, the two Fusilier Regiments were con--spicuous. Of the 7th Royal Fusiliers, with the laurels of Albuera fresh upon them, Robert Knowles had now become a member, joining it when it was actually in action, under the immediate direction of the greatest Commander of the day. Lord Wellington was then blockading Ciudad Rodrigo, and his headquarters were at Fuente Guinaldo. For six weeks, he had blockaded the Fortress, and, the garrison being in straits for food, Marshal Marmont resolved to pass in a convoy. With an Army of sixty thousand men, this was not a difficult operation, his adversary not being in a position to fight a general action. Wellington, however, drew in his forces which were scattered in and about El Bodon and Fuente Guinaldo. By so doing, he compelled Marmont to bring up his full strength before the revictualling of the beleaguered Fortress, which was accomplished on September 24th. On the following day, General Montbrun with fourteen Battalions of Infantry and a strong force of Cavalry advanced on Fuente Guinaldo, and thus began at El Bodon, six miles away, the action which was at its height when Lieutenant Knowles and his detachment arrived at Fuente Guinaldo.

The 3rd Division held the centre of the allied position

at El Bodon and Pastores, which were within three miles of Ciudad Rodrigo. The Light Division was on the right at Martiago on the Vadillo river, the 6th Division and a Brigade of Cavalry held the left. The pivot on which they all turned was Fuente Guinaldo, and at that spot was posted the 4th Division with which the 7th Royal Fusiliers were serving.

At daybreak on September 25th, General Montbrun, with fourteen Battalions of Infantry and three Brigades of Cavalry, crossed the Agueda river, and attacked at once our line of Cavalry picquets on the plain in the vicinity of El Bodon. The Frenchmen were met by the " fighting 3rd " Division under General Sir Thomas Picton. Taken in an exposed and isolated position and with his flank turned, Sir Thomas Picton retired from El Bodon and its vineyards, moving his column slowly across the plain, and, although repeatedly charged by the enemy's Cavalry, and fired at by six guns on his flank and rear, coolly and skilfully with- -drew his division. This retreat for six miles was a fine exhibition of nerve and calm self-possession on the part of the Commander, and of steadiness under fire on the part of his Officers and men.

When Wellington discovered the object of the French Commander, he sent the 5th Fusiliers, the 77th British, and the 21st Portuguese Regiments, and some Artillery, to occupy the hill over which ran the road to Fuente Guinaldo. The French Cavalry attacked the hill with

great vigour ; but, they were again and again driven down
the upper slopes. Montbrun brought up his Artillery and
soon made an impression, his Cavalry capturing some of
our guns. Meanwhile, our Cavalry, by charging too far,
became entangled in the vineyards. In this crisis, the
5th Fusiliers performed one of those extraordinary feats of
valour which were not infrequent in the campaigns under
Wellington. Led by Major Ridge, the 5th Fusiliers dashed
at the French Cavalry, and, sending them flying, re-
-captured the guns. It recalls the rout of the Cavalry at
Minden by six British regiments of infantry.

Lord Wellington ordered a general retirement to the
plain below, where the 5th and 77th formed one square,
and repulsed time after time the Cavalry that charged them.
All the forces, being re-united, now retired across the
plain to the position at Fuente Guinaldo, which Wellington
had defended by entrenchments and three redoubts. It
was during this retirement that the Fusilier Brigade—
the 7th and 23rd Fusiliers and the 48th Regiment—of
the 4th Division came up and covered the withdrawal
referred to by Lieutenant Knowles in his letter of October
7th, where he says, when we arrived, " the Fusilier Brigade
had marched about half an hour to cover the retreat of the
advance . . . . Our Regiment advanced in line with
the 23rd and 48th in close column on each flank, when,
having accomplished their object, they gradually returned
to their position, where we had the pleasure of joining them".

There is one incident in the combat at El Bodon, mentioned by Sir William Napier, which is particularly worthy of note : " it was in one of the Cavalry encounters that a French Officer, in the act of striking at the gallant Felton Harvey of the 14th Dragoons, perceived that he had only one arm, and with a rapid movement brought down his sword into a salute, and passed on ". Such were the courtesies between gallant men of both nations in this war.

Wellington in remaining at Fuente Guinaldo accepted a great risk which Napier describes as " above the rules of war ". With a disposable force of 14,000 men and in a moderate position, he confronted 60,000 men, remaining on the spot for thirty-six hours rather than abandon the famous " Light Division ". That risk was brought about by the deliberate failure of General Robert Craufurd to obey a written order to fall back upon Fuente Guinaldo. General Robert Craufurd, the ablest Lieutenant who ever served under Wellington, was the Commander of the " Light Division ", which was probably the most perfect fighting unit of Wellington's Armies. Receiving the order before 3 p.m. he marched only four miles, thus jeopardizing the safety of the whole force. Two Regiments of Picton's Division that were at Pastores, cut off by Montbrun's turning movement, made a march of fifteen hours and reached Fuente Guinaldo at night. Craufurd, without danger, could have done likewise. Wellington took the

C

risk. Craufurd, however, was blind to the offence of disregarding orders from his chief : for, he gave him the simple assurance that he was in no danger. " But it was, through your conduct that there was danger ", was the calm and stern reply. Still oblivious to his fault, Craufurd said to his Staff, referring to his chief, " he is d——d crusty to-day ".

The letter of Oct. 7th, continues, and describes the position at this moment :—

We remained under arms during the night. The Fusiliers formed the left of the line, where it was supposed the enemy would make their principal attack, which was fully expected early in the morning. Lord Wellington remained with us all the night and following day, while the enemy were amusing us by manœuvring in our front and bringing up their numerous reinforcements. About sunset Lord Wellington left us, and immediately the Army was on the move. Our Regiment brought up the rear of the Division, and marched about eleven o'clock, and did not halt until eleven o'clock the following morning at Aldea de Ponte.

At midnight on the 26th, the Army was in retreat, and by a skilful movement, Wellington united the whole twelve miles distant from Fuente Guinaldo, and behind the Villar Mayor.

As the next combat is the first in which Lieutenant Knowles received his baptism of fire, it may be of interest to give the disposition of the various Divisions. The right was held by the 5th Division at Aldea Velha, the 4th and Light Divisions and a Cavalry Brigade were in the centre in front of the village at Alfayates, and behind these, as a reserve, were the 3rd and 7th Divisions. On the left of the latter Division was a convent, whence the line was pro--longed by two Portuguese Brigades, the 6th Division and a Cavalry Brigade bringing the line to an end at Bismula.

In the front of the village of Aldea da Ponte, but leaning towards Furcalhous on the right of the position, was a line of our Cavalry picquets. Following in close pursuit, the French came up in force on the morning of the 27th, drove in the Cavalry picquets, and by ten o'clock were in possession of Aldea da Ponte.

At noon they attacked General Pakenham's Brigade of the Fourth Division, composed of the Fusilier Brigade of the 7th Royal Fusiliers, and the 23rd Fusiliers, and the 48th Regiment, which was posted on a range of heights. Wellington rode up at the critical moment, as he so frequently did, and directed the 7th to charge in line, supporting them on each flank with a Portuguese Regiment in column. Down they went, sending helter-skelter before them, the French, who then, entering a wood, tried to turn the position ; but, they were thwarted by our Artillery. Wellington, thereupon, acted on the offensive, and sent the 23rd and a Portuguese Regiment against the left of the French. They were successful, and the village was once more in the possession of the allies. A second party of the enemy coming up joined those who had attacked the village, making a fresh combined attack at five o'clock, and Aldea da Ponte was theirs for the second time. General Pakenham at the head of the two Fusilier Regiments drove them out again ; but, as the enemy were in consider--able force, and the light failing, and, as he knew that Wellington had fixed upon other ground for fighting a battle, he left Aldea da Ponte and re-occupied his position of the morning.

A description of the fight appears in the letter of October 7th, 1811. It is the account of a young enthusiastic Officer, fighting with his Regiment, thrilled with all the excitement and glow of a first battle.

The letter of Oct. 7th continues :—

About one o'clock the enemy made their appearance. It was a beautiful sight to see our Cavalry skirmishing with them, but before their superior numbers they gradu--ally retired upon us. Our Light Company, with the Light Companies of the 23rd, 48th, and a Company of Germans, acted in our front. Our Regiment was formed in square to receive their numerous Cavalry, which were rapidly advancing. The 23rd and 48th were also formed in square, a short distance upon our right, and about three thousand Portuguese were formed in line on some rising ground in our rear. Our Cavalry, about 2,000, formed on our left. This was the whole of the force we had to oppose to them on that day. Our Light Infantry gave a good account of the enemy's Cavalry, which retired in confusion. Several columns of Infantry continued to advance rapidly when we were suddenly ordered to form line. The fatigues of the night were forgot when Lord Wellington ordered the Fusiliers to charge the enemy. We advanced steadily against a heavy column of Imperial Guards, but they, perceiving our intention, retired in double quick time. Our Light Infantry poured in a dreadful fire amongst them, and numbers of them lay dead and dying on the field. They attempted to form on a rising ground opposite, where our Artillery did great execution. Our Cavalry and Light Infantry pursued them several miles, and were supported by a Regiment of Portuguese Cacadores. We naturally concluded that we should see no more of them that day, but the rascals had formed a plan to surprise our Light Infantry. About six o'clock we heard our Light Infantry very warmly engaged with them. General Packenham ordered the Fusiliers to fall in, and immediately marched us in the direction of the fire. My Captain was just gone on picket, so that I had the honor of com- -manding a company in action. We advanced in double quick time, and arrived when they had nearly surrounded the Light Infantry. Our right wing was ordered to charge, and to describe the eagerness of the men to close with them is impossible. General Packenham led us on (he is our Lieut.-Colonel—under such a man cowards would fight). Balls were flying about our ears like a hail-storm. He took off his hat, waved it in the air, and cried out " Lads ! Remember the Fusiliers ! ". The huzza that followed intimidated the French, and they ran too fast for our bayonets, but our fire mowed them down by dozens. We pursued them to the skirts of a wood, when we were ordered to retire. Our retiring encouraged the enemy, and the wood appeared like a flame with the fire they opened upon us. We retired in good order, the enemy not knowing the small number of men we had in the field, or they must inevitably have cut us to pieces, as we were afterwards informed by prisoners and deserters that they had eight thousand men in the wood, and the whole of the force we opposed to them did not exceed 500 men. The four companys we charged them with did not exceed 200 men. We had now time to look after our friends. We had four officers wounded, but none of them seriously. Many poor fellows fell on my right and left. One ball grazed my cap, another cut my canteen-strap in two, but I am happy to say there was not one billeted upon my body ".

During the night, Wellington withdrew his Army to a strong position on the Coa, which offered a very narrow frontage for attack. Marmont did not venture to test the strength of his opponent, but contented himself by placing a fresh Garrison in Ciudad Rodrigo. Wellington cantoned his Army along both banks of the Coa, giving them a much-needed rest, at the same time sending the Light Division and a Cavalry Brigade to watch Ciudad Rodrigo.

The letter of Oct. 7th ends, and gives the precise details of the movement of the writer's Regiment :—

On the morning of the 28th the greatest part of our Army was concentrated, but the enemy had received too good a lesson from our Division to follow the whole Army. We remained two nights in a large chestnut grove. We marched on the 1st, 2nd, and arrived at Alameda on the 3rd instant. On the 5th we marched to this place, Aldea de Bisboa. The whole Army, it is supposed, is in winter quarters, as rest is now absolutely necessary to recruit the Army. In the sick returns of last month there was up--wards of 22,000 British, and about one-half of the Portuguese Army.

The following letter, which is chiefly of a personal and domestic nature, gives the writer's estimation of the Spaniards and the Portuguese :—

To Mr. Robert Knowles.

Aldea de Bisboa, Oct. 8th, 1811.

My dear Father,—I write to you the first opportunity after the marches, counter-marches, and hard fighting we have had. I intended writing immediately after my arrival at the Army, but found it impossible to procure paper. They were all in such a state of confusion, and all our baggage was sent into the rear. I received mine on the 30th in the Chestnut Grove, and to-morrow the first mail for England leaves the Army. I was very unfortunate in my baggage being left behind. All the officers of the detachment were in the same situation ; when we received it, it had been pillaged. I had 35 dollars taken out of my portmanteau, besides a quantity of linen. The dollars was the balance due to the company I commanded. I am therefore under the necessity of again calling upon your generosity for the sum of ten pounds to be paid into the hands of Messrs. Greenwood & Co., Army agents, on account of Lieut. H. F. Devey,* with instructions to them to write to Mr. Devey the day they receive it. He has

* H. Fry Devey, Lieutenant, August 30th, 1807.

kindly offered to lend me the sum. Hope you will remit it to Messrs. Greenwood & Co. immediately, and write to me by the same post. I am much disappointed at not hearing from home since I left England, but suppose the reason to be that you are not aware the postage of all letters must be paid in England, which are going abroad. I will now give you a little of the country we passed through. From Figueras to Coimbra is a very fine corn country, and well cultivated. Coimbra is a large town, and has not suffered so much from the French as all the other towns. From Coimbra to Celorico it is a very rocky and mountainous country, but the valleys are full of olive trees, and the mountains covered with vineyards. We marched in the track the French Army retreated. They have destroyed all the villages, and there is scarcely a house with a roof on. The country appears quite de-
-populated. The little I have seen of the Spaniards I like much better than the Portuguese ; they are a much finer race of people, and take more pains to keep themselves clean. Their land is much better cultivated, and the French have not destroyed any of their villages. I must conclude, begging that you will write immediately on the receipt of this. Please to give my best respects to all my friends, particularly to my Couzin Lomax's ; give my best love to my sisters and brothers, and believe me,

Your sincerely affectionate Son,

Robt. Knowles, Lt.,

Royal Fusiliers.

Mr. Devey's address which I wish you to send to :—

Messrs. Greenwood and Co.,

Lieut. H. F. Devey,

7th Fusiliers,

British Army,

Portugal or Spain.

I promised to write to my Couzin John Lomax,* but have entirely forgot his address. Please to give it me in your next. If anything particularly interesting occurs I will write home.

P.S.—Lieut. Wray, of our Regiment, desires to be remembered to his brother, who is at Dr. Moor's.

Postmark, " C 22 OC. 22 1811."

A month elapses, when another letter, written to his father, tells of the movements of the Army in a com- -paratively quiet interlude :—

To Mr. Robert Knowles.

Villa de Saya, Nov. 5th, 1811.

Dear Father,—I wrote you last from Aldea de Bisboa on the 8th ult., and on the 12th we were moved to this village, where we remained quiet until Saturday last, when we were suddenly ordered to march in the direction of Quinaldo (you will recollect it is the place I mentioned in my last as having joined our Regiment). We were all of us ignorant of the business we were going upon until we arrived at the end of our march, when we were much mortified to hear that John Bull was too late, and we were ordered to march back to our old quarters on the following day. It was intended that our Division should intercept a large convoy of stores that was going to the relief of Ciudad Rodrigo, escorted by about five thousand men, but the enemy had accomplished their purpose the day before we marched. There has nothing interesting occurred since my last letter. You will see in the papers

---

* Son of Ellen Knowles who married Richard Lomax, of Harwood, and was a widow in 1779.

an account of the capture by the Spaniards of the Governor of Ciudad Rodrigo. He was marched prisoner through this village. The French lately murdered some Spanish prisoners, and they naturally retaliated by murdering some Frenchmen that fell into their hands a few days ago. They have also detected a French spy, and were so kind as to make us a present of a hind quarter, which is hung up a short distance from my billet. A few days ago I visited Almieda. The town is destroyed, and the forti--fications are very much injured, but Lord Wellington is now repairing the works. On Sunday I had a very fine view of Ciudad Rodrigo, as I walked within three miles of the town, but hope to have a nearer inspection the ensuing spring. I am sorry to say I have not received a letter from home since I left England, but am daily expecting that pleasure. We have great news from General Hill's Army, but you will see the particulars before we have them, as the only accounts we expect to receive will be through the English papers. On the receipt of the first letter from home I shall again write. Remember me to my sisters, brothers, and all enquiring friends, and believe me,

Your affectionate Son,

R. Knowles, Lieut., R.F.

Postmark, " Lisbon, De. 13. 1811."

The Governor of Ciudad Rodrigo, to whose capture reference is made, was General Renaud, who had im--prudently left a Fortress with a weak escort, and he and his whole party, with 200 head of cattle, were captured by the Spanish Cavalry under Julian Sanchez. The loss of the cattle was of more serious consequence to the Garrison than the loss of the Governor. The position of the Commander was taken by the next senior Officer, but, the loss of the cattle could not be made good.

Then, as now, Armies in the field, fighting in an extended area, had less knowledge of what was occurring in other Divisions than had people living at a distance.

General Hill was operating at this time in Estremadura, and his swift and brilliant surprise and dispersion of the force under General Gerard in Arroyo dos Molinos, deservedly established his reputation as a Commander ; this is the " great news " mentioned in the last paragraph but one of the letter of November 5th. In this affair, out of 3,000, only 600 Frenchmen escaped.

In the letter of December 3rd, 1811, there is no ex--aggeration of the hardships and privations of the Army at that time. Napier says, " the pay of the Army was three months in arrears, and the supplies, brought up with difficulty, were very scanty ; half and quarter rations were often served, and sometimes the troops were without any bread for three days consecutively." The labour of preparing for a siege was arduous. It was mid-winter and the cantonments were unhealthy from incessant rain. It is not surprising, therefore, that there were 20,000 men in hospital.

To Mr. Robert Knowles.

Barba de Porca, Dec. 3rd, 1811.

My dear Father,—I am happy to acknowledge the receipt of my brother's letter of the 30th Sept. Since I

last wrote you on the 4th ult. we have had some very
severe marches.   On the 11th, four companys of our
Regiment marched from Villa de Serva to this village,
which is situated upon the Aqueda.   Here is the celebrated
pass by which the French garrison of Almeida escaped.
The river runs rapidly, and the rocks on each side are
tremendous.   It is really astonishing how they succeeded.
On the 23rd, in the morning, we had only ten minutes'
notice to march in the direction of Ciudad Rodrigo.   We
joined our Regiment in the evening at Gallegas, after a
march of twenty-five miles.   Early in the morning we
proceeded on our march to Camp Ello, a miserable village
about six miles on the right of Ciudad Rodrigo.   Near this
place the enemy must pass if they relieved that fortress.
Here we remained until the 29th, when we were ordered
to return to our old quarters.   The five days we were at
Camp Ello we only received one pound of biscuit, and
fatigue partys were ordered into the woods to gather
acorns as a substitute for bread.   In this starving state we
had only twenty cottages to quarter seven hundred men.
You will agree with me when I say very few men in England
would envy our situation.   On the 1st instant two officers
from each Regiment were ordered to examine the passes
over the Aqueda, so as to enable them to conduct the
different Regiments in the most expeditious manner to
any point that may be required.   The enemy's convoys
are now at Salamanca, waiting a favourable opportunity
of proceeding to the relief of Ciudad Rodrigo, but I believe
they will find it a difficult matter unless they collect their
immense Army.   The deserters from the enemy are very
numerous, particularly from Ciudad Rodrigo.   The morn-
-ing we marched to this village we met one officer and
twenty-eight men ; those from Ciudad Rodrigo say that
the garrison is on half allowance.   My brother mentions

the return of our 2nd Battalion to England, but they are now ordered to Jersey. At present there is no probability of me being ordered to join them. I returned the letters I received from Mr. Wood when at Lisbon, under cover of a letter I wrote you. Chadk. says Mr. James Orrel is anxious to hear from his brother. I mentioned in my last that he is in General Hill's Army in the Alentigo. I am anxiously waiting an answer to my letter of the 8th Oct. I also wrote you on the 4th ult. No doubt you have received both by this time. Our officers and men continue sickly. In our last advance we left nine officers in the rear, but I am thankful my health continues good ; better if possible than when in England. We have no news here that is interesting, but are all expecting to advance. I will there--fore conclude. Give my best respects to all enquiring friends. Remember me to my sisters and brothers, and believe me,

Your affectionate Son,

Robt. Knowles,

Lieut. Royal Fusiliers.

P.S.—My brother mentions that Startem has been to school to John Lee, but is a great blockhead. I therefore am sorry to hear that he is a favorite with my sister, but I trust he will provide another dog against my return, and send it to the same master. You must not forget to remem--ber me to John Lee, and tell him there is plenty of game. One of his dogs would be invaluable if with the Army. A spaniel which he would not harbour was yesterday sold for 100 dollars.

The next letter home brings New Year's wishes for " every pleasure this world can afford ".

Villa de Serva, Dec. 31st, 1811.

Dear Father,—The Army is still in the same quarters, but we are daily expecting a move. It is supposed that Ciudad Rodrigo will be Lord Wellington's first object, as he is making preparations for a siege. Detachments from each Regiment in the 4th Division are employed making gabions and fascines for the erection of batterys, and the battering-train have orders to be in readiness to march at an hour's notice. He has also thrown a bridge over the Aqueda about eight miles from this village and six from Ciudad Rodrigo. The French have detached two Divisions of their Army, and have evacuated Placentia. If we do advance I hope our Regiment will be in the front, as I would prefer fighting to lying in the trenches at this season. The Spaniards annoy the French a great deal in this part of the country. General Mina alone destroyed seven thou--sand of them the last month. I have not heard from home since the 30th Sept., but suppose your letters must have miscarried. I did not neglect drinking your good health on Christmas Day, nor that of all my absent friends, but must say I envied their situation sitting by a fireside with their bellys full of Christmas pyes, but if they are feasting upon all the luxurys England can afford I shall enjoy them the more when I return, with this satisfaction, that I have fought for my country abroad. While writing the above I received a pressing invitation from Capt. King, of our Regiment, to dine with him and Major Des--pard. The only news I can give you is that we shall break ground before Ciudad Rodrigo on the 13th inst., for you must know it is now the New Year, and I have the satis--faction to wish you every pleasure this world can afford. If I do not hear from you in answer to a letter of the 8th October in a few days, I shall be under the necessity of drawing a bill upon you for £20. The last letter I wrote you was of the 3rd ult., but have no doubt you have received it by this time. The Army is not so sickly as it was when I last wrote, and it gives me great pleasure to say I remain in perfect health. I will again write you if any--thing particular occurs. In the meantime, I remain,

Your affectionate Son,

R. Knowles, Lieut., Royal Fusiliers.

Postmark, " Lisbon, Ja. 22. 1812."

1 8 1 2 .

The New Year was heralded in for the Allied Army by the capture of Ciudad Rodrigo, which Wellington had persistently blockaded.

The foregoing letter tells of making preparation for the siege in connection with which it gives even a date ! The 1st, 3rd, 4th, and Light Divisions were selected for this duty, each Division taking its turn in rotation. They had to cross a river, wading sometimes up to the waist, to reach the trenches. The winter was unusually severe, and the Troops suffered great hardships. On January 8th, the Light Division, making a circuit, took up a position distant three miles from the Fortress. In the evening that distinguished soldier, Colonel John Colborne, at the head of two Companies from each of the Regiments of the Light Division, carried by assault the palisaded redoubt Francisco, which was close to the " Greater Tesson," the farther of the two ridges on the north side. The operation was well managed by the stormers, whose loss was but trifling, and during the night they made a parallel of 600 yards.

On the 10th, the 4th Division were in the trenches, and opened communications from the parallel to the batteries. By the 19th, the breaches became practicable ; and, as there was a probability that Marmont might attempt to relieve the fortress, Lord Wellington decided to carry it by assault. His final order showed the confidence which he had in his soldiers. It ended with the imperative command— " Ciudad Rodrigo must be stormed this evening". The storming was committed to the 3rd and Light Divisions, and the Portuguese under General Pack. The 4th Division was held in reserve.

The operation was divided into three attacks, right, centre, and left, with a false attack upon the St. Jago gate, at the opposite side of the town. The troops in the right attack were to cross the Agueda river, and escalade an outwork in front of the Castle. Colonel O'Toole of the Cacadores was in command. The centre attack was to be made by the 3rd Division, Major Manners commanding the storming-party of five hundred Volunteers, and Major George Napier commanding three hundred men of the Light Division.

All were in their appointed places when the attack was prematurely commenced on the right. The storming parties rushed, with astonishing speed under a heavy fire, into the breaches. The main body of the 3rd Division were the first to get in, and for a short time they drove the French before them ; but, they were held up by a tempest of grape and musket-fire, and by the filling-up of the passages with the bodies of the dead and wounded. The stormers of the Light Division jumped into the dark ditch, eleven feet deep, and soon found their way up to the smaller breach, which was so narrow that one gun was sufficient to block it. The Officers dashed into it followed by their men, while the supports followed rapidly, and at this point the Fortress was won.

The 43rd enfiladed the defenders, and the explosion of the Magazines at the same time helped the 3rd Division to get in at the centre, the Portuguese on the right gaining also the positions assigned to them. For a short time there was some fighting in the streets ; but, soon all was over, and the Governor, who was in the Castle, surrendered his sword to Lieutenant Gurwood, the leader of the "forlorn hope " of the Light Division.

The French lost 300 killed and 1,500 wounded, while 150 guns with much ammunition were captured. The Allies lost 90 Officers and 1,200 men killed and wounded ; of these, 60 Officers and 650 men were killed, or wounded, at the breaches.

Among the slain were Generals Craufurd and Mackinnon. The former was mortally wounded while directing the attack on the lesser breach, and died a few

D

days afterwards. " A man of great ability " is his description by one who loved him not. He was a stern dis--ciplinarian and a capable Commander, both liked and feared by the men of the Light Division, whom he had brought as fighting soldiers to the highest point of perfection. In seven minutes the Light Division was packed and under arms ready to march or take its place in a line of battle : and this, not on special occasions, but always. It is the leader-ship that tells, and the 43rd, 52nd, and 95th (now the Rifle Brigade) Regiments were indeed fortunate to have been trained by two Commanders of the eminence of Sir John Moore and General Robert Craufurd. The per--sonality of Craufurd remained with the Light Division long after he had died. The mortal remains of that in--trepid warrior were laid in the breach of the bastion that he had won, and it still bears his name. General Mackin--non was beloved by all who knew him, including Napoleon, with whom, strange to relate, he had been a friend in his youth.

Sir William Napier, who was present with his Regiment, the 43rd, says : " There died many gallant men, amongst others a Captain of the 45th, of whom it has been felicitously said, that three Generals and seventy other Officers had fallen, but the soldiers, fresh from the strife, only talked of Hardyman ".

Many more details are given in the two following letters.

To Mr. Robert Knowles.

Castelheo, Jany. 20th, 1812.

My dear Father,—It gives me great pleasure to inform
you that Ciudad Rodrigo has surrendered to our arms.
In my last I mentioned the probability of our besieging
that fortress. On the 8th instant we marched from our
cantoonment to St. Felius Chico, near which place we
crossed the river Aqueda. The same evening the Light
Division took by storm a strong outwork within 400 yards
of Ciudad Rodrigo, and broke ground about the same
distance from the fortress. On the 9th, the 1st Division
relieved the Light ; on the 10th we relieved the 1st, and
on the 11th the 3rd Division relieved us. The whole
duties of the siege have been carried on by the four Divisions
I have mentioned. The works were carried on briskly
under showers of shot from the enemy, and three battery's
were completed, and the guns opened about three o'clock
on the evening of the 14th instant. I was on duty in one
of the battery's at the time, and consider myself a lucky
fellow to escape without a scratch, as my party had the
dangerous duty of opening the embrazures for the guns,
and the enemy's fire was directed altogether at us. A very
fine young man, a lieut. in the Engineers, was mortally
wounded when standing by my side. Our guns played
their part well, and in one hour silenced all the enemy's
guns in their front. Our guns continued to batter in
breach until the 19th, when the breach was reported
practicable, and the Light Division ordered to assist the
Division on duty to storm the place. Our Division was
relieved on the 19th by the Third, but the Fusilier Brigade
was detained until three o'clock, and we fully expected to
share with the Third and Light Divisions the honor of
storming the town, and were much annoyed at being

ordered into quarters at this village. It is the most pain-
-ful part of my duty to state the loss it is supposed we have
sustained in storming the town, which commenced about
seven o'clock in the evening. The 45th and 88th Regts.
were the first to enter the breach, and, of course, have
suffered the most. It is said we lost about 500 men, in-
-cluding about thirty-five officers. Genl. Crawford is
mortally wounded, *Col. Coborne, of the 52nd, killed.
Genl. Mackinnon, of the Guards, was killed by the blowing
up of a magazine after the town had surrendered ; but,
you will see the particulars of the siege and the [loss] we
have sustained in the Gazette. I believe our Regt. in the
whole of the siege has not lost more than fifteen men. We
fully expect to march to-morrow, whether to the front or
return to our old quarters is uncertain. The garrison of
Ciudad Rodrigo are marched as prisoners to Almeada
to-day. I am in great haste to be in time for the post,
therefore must conclude by subscribing myself,

Your affectionate Son,

R. Knowles,

Lieut. R.F.

P.S.—I have not received a letter from home since the
30th Sept., and we have accounts from England up to the
31st Dec. You must be aware, as I mentioned in a former
letter, that the postage of all letters from abroad must be
paid in England, otherwise they will not be forwarded.

---

* The writer was here in error, as Colonel Colborne survived until
1863. Colonel Colborne was for many years known as Sir John
Colborne, until he became Field-Marshal Lord Seaton. A distinguished
soldier who, upon many occasions, proved himself to be capable of turn-
-ing the fate of a battle. At Waterloo, though it never received any
official recognition, he made the critical and determining attack on the
Old Guard. Lord Seaton died in 1863.—L. K.

In a letter, dated one month later, there are given further details connected with the taking of Ciudad Rod--rigo. There were twenty deserters found in the Fortress : some were shot, some were otherwise punished, and some were forgiven :—

To Mr. Robert Knowles.

Almada, Feby. 18th, 1812.

Dear Father,—After the lapse of several months I have the pleasure to acknowledge the receipt of a letter from my brother of so late a date as the 29th ult. I have wrote you since the fall of Ciudad Rodrigo, since which time there has nothing particular occurred. We marched a few days ago from Castlejos through Ciudad Rodrigo to Carpio, and yesterday we came to this village, but I do not suppose we shall remain here many days, as it is believed the greatest part of the Army will gradually move to the South, and then we expect to be amused by the seige of Badajos. We have had a hard day's work, the whole of our Division having been assembled to see the sentence of a General Court Martial put in force on two deserters, who were taken in Ciudad Rodrigo. They were sentenced to be shot ; it was the most awful sight I ever beheld. My brother asks if any of the Bolton lads are present. I only know one that is with the Regt., of the name of Robinson. I will make enquirys after the others, and write you in my next. He also asks after two men of the name of Jackson ; if he will write me when they were enlisted, and where they come from, I will make enquiry after them. I was obliged to break off my letter here to perform the most melancholy part of my duty. I was call'd upon to superin--tend the funeral of a poor fellow in my Company. It would astonish some of my acquaintances in England to see me acting in the place of a clergyman, reading the Burial Service, etc. Our Regt. is still very sickly, and I am sorry to say the mortality is very great, numbers of our poor fellows dying after three or four days' sickness. I mentioned in some of my letters that I should be under the necessity of drawing a bill upon you for £20, but the kindness of a friend has rendered it unnecessary, but hope you will on receipt of this pay into the hands of Messrs. Greenwood and Co., Army Agents, the sum of £20 to be placed to the account of Lieut. H. F. Devey, of our Regt., and desire the Agents to write him on the receipt of it. I beg you will not lose any time in lodging the money, and be particular in desiring them to write to him without loss of time, as it will be his only receipt for it. I shall anxiously wait an answer to this letter, but in the meantime be so good as to remember me to all enquiring friends, and my best respects to my brothers and sisters.

Your sincerely affectionate Son,
Robt. Knowles, Lieut.,
Fusiliers.

THE THIRD SIEGE OF BADAJOZ.

The third attempt to capture Badajoz, a Spanish town and fortress on the Portuguese border, began on March 15th, 1812, when Marshal Beresford invested the fortress with the 3rd, 4th, and Light Divisions, and a Portuguese Brigade, a force in all of 15,000 men. Badajoz was de--fended by 5,000 French, Hessian, and Spanish soldiers under a resolute, resourceful French officer, General

Armand Phillipon, who had stored provisions both for the citizens and for the garrison, sufficient to last three months : but, he was short of ammunition.

The town stands where a small stream, the Rivillas, runs into the Guadiano, and the defences consisted of curtains and bastions, from 23 to 30 feet high, with counter--scarps. There was a castle with numerous outworks, including San Roque, the Picurina, a redoubt 400 yards from the town, the Pardaleras, between the Guadiano and Rivillas and 200 yards from the ramparts, but connected therewith and defended by powerful batteries : these were all on the left bank of the Guadiano. On the right bank stood the Fort of San Cristobal, which overlooked the interior of the Castle, and on the western side of it was the redoubt of San Vincente, with three forts, which were mined. The arch of the bridge of San Roque was built up to make an inundation, 18 feet deep. These, briefly, were the main defences.

In the two sieges of 1811, the plan of operations was to assault the castle, at the South-Eastern corner of the fortress, and the redoubt Cristobal. On this occasion, for various reasons, it was decided to attack the bastions of Trinidad and Santa Maria ; but, before this could be attempted, the Picurina hill had to be stormed and captured. Preparatory for this, the first communication and parallel were made on March 17th, and, one week later, on March 25th, after stupendous difficulties caused by floods and other untoward circumstances, all was ready for the attack. The redoubt was stronger than its appearance indicated ; but, in the night of the 25th, General Kempt with 500 men of the 3rd Division carried it by assault, when 319 Officers and men were killed or wounded.

Time was running against Wellington. Marshal Soult with an army was approaching him. He sent, therefore, General Graham's Division to take up a position at Albuera to which he purposed withdrawing all but an investing force, and there to offer battle, should the necessity arise. But Wellington's soldiers were fiercely eager for the fray, and, the breaches being considered practicable, an order went forth that the fortress was to be stormed in the night of April 6th. General Picton's Division, " the fighting 3rd", was to cross the Rivillas stream, and escalade the castle wall, while Major Wilson of the 48th Regiment, with the Guards of the trenches, was to attack San Roque. This was the right attack. In the centre, the 4th and Light Divisions under General Colville and Colonel Barnard were to assault and force the breaches. To the 4th Division was assigned the Trinidad, and to the Light Division the bastion of Santa Maria. Each attack was preceded by forlorn hopes and storming parties of 500 men. The 5th Division while making a feint on Pardaleras were to carry the bastion of San Vincente.

On that dark evening there was but little to show the volcanic forces that lay hidden within the fortress. An

occasional light, and the voices of the sentinels on the
ramparts passing the report that all was well, gave no
indication or hint to the besiegers that the garrison were
alert and prepared with every means that the ingenuity
of a capable and experienced Commander could devise for
the destruction of their assailants. The British longed for
the hour when they would be let loose at the Fortress :
they were galled by the prolonged restraint, and they hated
sieges. The digging and excavating, the long hours in
crouching attitudes in wet and muddy trenches, exhausted
their patience and irritated them, until their temper was
one of suppressed, frenzied, anger. Wellington's order
was for a simultaneous attack at 10 o'clock, but a fire-ball
or " carcase", to use the soldiers' term, thrown from the
castle disclosed the position and readiness of the 3rd
Division, and they were consequently obliged to make
an attack, premature by half an hour. The 4th and Light
Divisions were compelled to move at the same time,
silently and quickly, to the breaches. Major Wilson's
detachment consisted of the guards of the trenches, and
with these were fifty men of the Royal Fusiliers under
Lieutenant Knowles. This was the first party to effect
the capture of any portion of the defence, and what
happened is best told by Lieutenant Knowles in a letter
to his father dated June 19th, 1812.

The 3rd Division crossed the Rivillas, but were met
with a heavy stream of musketry fire. Rushing forward

they placed the scaling ladders against the walls of the castle, and rapidly ascended, only to meet with a terrible fire. The ladders were pushed from the walls, heavy blocks of wood, crushing all beneath, were thrown upon them. They fell back to the shelter of the hill, where they were re-formed. Colonel Ridge of the 5th Fusiliers, in a loud voice called upon his men to follow him, and rushing forward placed a ladder against a lower part of the wall, near an embrasure : another Officer, Ensign Canch*, placed a second ladder close to the first : and, in a moment, both Officers were on the ramparts, their men crowding after them. The French, astounded by such daring, were driven into the town, and the castle was won, but it was not to be retained if the enemy could prevent it. Bringing up their reserves, they attacked the castle at the main town entrance, but were repulsed, at the cost of the life of that gallant leader, Colonel Ridge, who was shot through the bars of the gate.

Glancing at that part of this terrible fight, where the Light and 4th Divisions were engaged, it is necessary to take the main incidents of the struggle of the two Divisions in their proper sequence. The stormers of the Light Division, led by the heroic Major O'Hara, rushed

---

* Ensign Thomas Canch was not promoted Lieutenant until May, 1813. He became Adjutant of the 5th Fusiliers in the same year, and that position he held until 1830, when he was promoted Captain. Seventeen years a Subaltern ! This is an illustration of the injustice that was prevalent in the Army, under the system of promotion by purchase.

forward, jumped into the ditch, and placed their ladders against the walls of the Santa Maria. A bright flashing light, coming as from the earth, illuminated the whole scene, and showed to the defenders who were crowded on the ramparts, the heavy swinging columns of the two British Divisions, following their respective storming--parties. Suddenly, there was a deafening explosion of shell, powder, and powder-barrels, which hurled the storming-parties to atoms. The Light Division were for a moment appalled by the spectacle ; but, rending the air with a loud angry shout, they leaped into a ditch. At this moment, the 4th Division came running up, and poured in to the sunken fray. In one place the bottom of the ditch had been scooped out, and filled with water, and into this one hundred men fell and were drowned. They belonged to the two Fusilier Regiments, the 7th and 23rd— the men of Albuera. Those who followed turned to the left and came on the face of the unfinished ravelin. This was mistaken for the breach : but, between the ravelin and the ramparts there was a yawning chasm. Again baffled, there was great confusion as the two Divisions crowded in the ravelin. They made an unexpected rush for the breach, but there across the top glittered a range of sword-blades, keen-edged on both sides, firmly fixed in heavy beams. It was impossible to gain a firm foot-hold, as loose planks studded with nails were laid in the narrow pathway, causing each man who tried to stand on them to fall. The attempt to force an entrance was made again and again. Colonel Macleod of the 43rd was shot in the breach. Two hours of this fruitless carnage convinced the Officers and men that they could not get through the breach in the Trinidad, or the Santa Maria. The main attack had failed and 2,000 men had fallen in the effort.

About midnight, Lord Wellington ordered the two Divisions to retire from the breaches, so as to prepare for a second assault. The 3rd Division still held the castle. General Walker's Brigade of the 5th Division had escaladed the bastion of San Vincente and, fighting their way along the ramparts and into the town, had captured three bastions as they went. The fighting in the town continued for some time, then once more it turned to the ramparts, where its course was checked, and then it turned again back into the town. Finding that the British were momentarily increasing their numbers in the town, the French withdrew from the defence of the breaches, and Badajoz was won, and won, not by the troops of the main attack, but by the 3rd Division which forced its way into the castle—an in--spiration of Sir Thomas Picton, who begged that he might be allowed to assault the castle—, by Walker's Brigade at San Vincente, and, in some degree, by the guards of the trenches under Wilson.

General Phillipon, who was wounded, surrendered on the following morning.

In this assault, no less than 3,500 British Officers and men

fell, and, of these, 60 Officers and 700 men were killed
on the spot. At the breaches the 4th and Light Division
each lost 1,200 men, and of the 7th Fusiliers, 5 Officers and
44 men were killed, and 13 Officers and 121 men were
wounded.

This letter, undated, but written on April 7th, 1812,
the day after the capture of the town of Badajos, gives
some vivid personal experiences :—

Stamped, " Packet Letter, Plymouth ", and " 2/6 ".

To Mr. Robert Knowles.
Camp before Badajos.

Dear Father,—It gives me great pleasure to be able to
write you after the bloody business on the night of the
6th. At the commencement of the business I had the
honourable command of a party of 40 men of our Regt.,
which, with others of the Division, to the number of 150,
under the command of Capt. Horton, of the 23rd, were
ordered to storm †[the Raveline], a strong outwork about
100 yards from the town, defended on one side by water
and a wall around it about 24 feet in height. After being
exposed for half an hour to the hottest fire I was ever under,
we succeeded in placing one ladder against the wall, by which
my party entered. A Corporal was the first who got into
the Fort, and was immediately killed. I was the third
man who mounted the ladder. On leaping into the place I
was knocked down by a shower of grape which broke my

† The words in brackets are almost illegible, probably by reason
of the wounded hand.

sabre into a hundred pieces. I providentially escaped without any serious injury, although my clothes were torn from my back. My sword hand is much cut and bruised, which accounts for my bad writing, and my right side is a little bruised. As I mentioned to you before, my sword was broken in pieces. I therefore picked up my Corporal's firelock, and with the assistance of eight or ten men who had now got into the Fort, I charged along the ramparts, destroying or disarming all who opposed us. The French Garrison consisted of 150 men, but we only took and destroyed about 60, the remainder made their escape to the town. We found 5 guns in the Fort. After properly securing the Fort, we advanced to assist in the attack of the town. You will see the particulars of the whole business in the Gazette, and as my hand is very painful I must conclude. Suffice it to say our Regt. is cut to pieces ; we lost 5 officers kill'd and 12 wounded ; our wounded officers will leave the Camp this morning, when there will be only ten officers with the Regt., and scarcely one of them without a bruise. The post will leave the Camp at 10 o'clock, but I will write you by the next. Please to remember me to all enquiring friends, and my best respects for my dear sisters and brothers, and believe me,

Your affectionate Son,

R. Knowles, Lt., Fusiliers.

P.S.—Lieut. Wray, whom my brother has often men--tioned, is one of the unfortunate officers who fell in the breach of Badajos.

Sir William Napier concludes the narrative of this assault with a splendid testimony :—

" Let any man picture to himself this frightful carnage taking place in a space of less than one hundred square yards. Let him consider that the slain died not all suddenly, nor by one manner of death ; that some perished by steel, some by shot, some by water, that some were crushed and mangled by heavy weights, some trampled upon, some dashed to pieces by the fiery explosions ; that for hours this destruction was endured without shrinking, and that the town was won at last ;—Let any man consider this and he must admit that a British Army bears with it an awful power. Who shall do justice to the bravery of the soldiers ? the noble emulation of the Officers ? who shall measure out the glory of Ridge, of Macleod, of Nicholas, or of O'Hara of the 95th, who perished on the breach at the head of the stormers, and with him nearly all the volunteers of that desperate service. No action, no age ever sent forth braver troops to battle than those who stormed Badajoz".

O'Hara, when leaving camp for the assault, remarked, " a Lieutenant-Colonel, or dead-meat, to-morrow".

THE BATTLE OF SALAMANCA.

The Fortress of Ciudad Rodrigo fell in January, and Badajoz in April, and yet the campaign of this year did not begin until June when both Armies were assembled for a mighty contest in the open field.

The Royal Fusiliers, with the 4th Division, crossed the Tagus on April 20th, and were quartered at Valongas. The movements of the Regiment and indeed of the Army, is well described in the letter from Salamanca of June 19th, 1812, which is a connecting link in the events between the fall of Badajoz, and the movements leading up to the defeat of the French at Salamanca. It gives, moreover, a precise narrative of the part taken by the detachment under the command of Lieutenant Knowles in the storming and capture of San Roque :—

To Mr. Robert Knowles.

Camp near Salamanca,
June 19th, 1812.

Dear Father,—I wrote you last on the 7th April, the day after the storming of Badajos, and promised to write you again by the next post, but the nature of the wound in my hand rendered it impossible, although it did not prevent me marching with my Regt. to the North of Portugal. On our arrival at Valango I was attacked with a slow fever, from which I barely recovered when we marched from those quarters on the 5th instant. I was sent to Celonio, in charge of the sick of the Division, but on my arrival obtained leave to rejoin my Regt., and by making a few days forced marches I joined them in camp near Ciudad Rodrigo on the 12th inst. On the 13th, 14th, 15th, and 16th we marched toward Salamanca. On the night of the 16th the enemy evacuated the town, but have left a garrison in two convents which .they have fortified. Our battery are in a forward state, and it is expected will open upon their works to-morrow morning. The 6th Division and two German Regts. are quartered in the town, and carry on the dutys of the siege. The Light Division and 3rd Division are in the front of us, about two miles. Ours

and the 5th Division are encamped on the banks of the
Tormes, a most beautiful river which runs close by the town
of Salamanca. The 1st and 7th Divisions are on our right ;
they are also encamped on the banks of the river. I
yesterday went over to see the town. The Cathedral
surpasses in grandeur anything I ever saw, and the town
excels in every respect any that I have seen in this country.
As soon as we have taken the enemy's works at Salamanca,
it is supposed we shall advance with the greatest rapidity
into the heart of Spain, as it is supposed Marmont cannot
collect an Army strong enough to fight us. I mentioned
to you in my last that I was not with my Regt. at
the storming of Badajos, but on duty in the trenches.
Major Wilson, 48th Regt., received orders to attack with
300 men Fort St. Roque (or the Raveline). Our Regt.
furnished 50 men for that duty. I apply'd and succeeded
in obtaining the command of them. When the 3rd Division
commenced their attack upon the Castle we advanced to
the Raveline, and after considerable difficulty we succeeded
in placing one ladder against the wall, about 24 feet high.
A Corporal of mine was the first to mount it, and he was
kill'd at the top of it. I was the third or fourth, and when
in the act of leaping off the wall into the Fort I was knocked
down by a discharge from the enemy, the handle of my
sabre broke into a hundred pieces, my hand disabled,
and at the same time I received a very severe bruise on
my side, and a slight wound, a piece of lead (having pene-
-trated through my haversack, which was nearly filled with
bread, meat, and a small stone brandy-bottle for the use
of the trenches during the night) lodged upon one side of my
ribs, but without doing me any serious injury. I recovered
myself as soon as possible, and by the time seven or eight
of my brave fellows had got into the Fort, I huzzaed and
charged along the ramparts, killing or destroying all who

E

opposed us.   I armed myself with the first Frenchman's
firelock I met with, and carried it as well as I was able under
my arm.   The greater part of my party having joined me,
we charged into the body of the Fort, when they all cried
out " Prisoners".   I forgot to mention to you the plan of
attack : 150 men were to escalade on each side, but by some
mistake they all attacked on the contrary side to what I
did, and I have the satisfaction to state that my party let
them all in at the gates.   All the British troops from the
trenches were ordered to support the 3rd Division in the
Castle, and Major Wilson gave me charge of the Fort,
with the remains of my party.   From the end of a wall
where I seated myself, I had a fine view of the different
attacks upon the town.   We secured about 60 prisoners,
who had concealed themselves in different parts of the
Fort, and we kill'd and wounded about twenty-five.   My
party suffered severely.   My sergeant and corporal were
kill'd, and about twenty-five men kill'd and wounded.*

The forts at Salamanca were captured on June 27th.
Seven hundred prisoners, thirty guns, provisions, and a secure
passage over the Tormes, were the reward of this success,
which was achieved ten days earlier than Marshal Marmont
thought possible.   Fearing to give his opponent any
advantage from a chosen position, Marmont retired,
followed by Wellington.   On July 18th, the 4th and Light
Divisions with a Brigade of Cavalry were engaged all day
with several French columns, and the 7th Fusiliers had
twenty men wounded.   There now occurred one of those

* The remainder of this letter is missing.

instances of strange friendliness between contending Armies which were not infrequent in the Peninsular Cam-
-paign. The British Divisions were marching in column, the Light Division being nearest the French, but separated from them by the German Cavalry. Both Armies were moving at a rapid pace for the Guarena river, and the Officers on each side, pointing their swords or waving their hands in courtesy, alternated their salutations with loud commands, while they passed from front to rear of their men, to quicken the pace towards the common goal. Such were the civilities between the Officers of both Armies.

On the morning of July 22nd, Marshal Marmont brought more troops within the zone of fire, and occupied a wooded height on which stood an old Chapel. Close by were two hills called the Arapiles, by which name the battle of Salamanca is known to the Spaniards to this day. Welling-
-ton seized the farther of the two, while the French occupied the second, and at the same time he sent some companies of the Guards and Royal Fusiliers to drive the enemy out of the village of Arapiles. Wellington, who himself witnessed this action, was so pleased with the manner in which the Fusiliers did their work that he mentioned the name of Captain Crowder in his despatch. The 4th Division was in position on a ridge behind the village, while the 5th and 6th were drawn into the inner slopes of the Arapiles. The 3rd Division under General Pakenham was in a wood near Aldes Tejada, where they were hidden from the enemy,

while they commanded the main road to Ciudad Rodrigo. The interval between the 3rd and 4th Divisions was occupied by Bradford's Portuguese Brigade, the Spaniards, and the British Cavalry.

Wellington's position was now a strong one, and his hope was that Marmont would attack him. At 2 p.m., when at dinner, he received word that the French were moving towards the road to Ciudad Rodrigo. At once, he mounted his horse and earnestly watched the moving columns of the enemy. At 3 p.m., when their left was entirely separated from the centre, he said, " Marmont's good genius has forsaken him ", and he issued the orders that brought on the battle. The 5th Division formed on the right of the 4th Division, and, with the Portuguese and Cavalry, presented a front to the enemy. The 6th and 7th Divisions, British Cavalry and Spaniards, prolonged the line in the direction of the 3rd Division. When these dispositions were completed, Wellington ordered the 3rd Division, with 12 guns and a Brigade of Cavalry to cross the enemy's line of march. To his brother-in-law, General Pakenham, the Commander of the 3rd Division in Picton's absence, he said, pointing to the column of Thomières, " Ned, do you see those fellows ? Throw your Division into column and drive them to the devil". The reply was, " Yes : but, let me grasp that conquering right hand". As Pakenham's attack developed, the remainder of the first line was ordered to attack. When Marmont saw the 3rd Division break across the path of his column on the Ciudad Rodrigo road, he was dismayed. At 5 o'clock, Pakenham began the battle by falling on the front of the French column as it emerged from a wood, while his guns took it in flank. Disconnected, and with many men still in the wood, it was taken at a great disadvantage, and Pakenham pushed home his success with terrible force. The 4th Division, under General Lowry Cole, deployed into line and, with the 5th, passing the Arapiles village and crossing some heavy ploughed land under a storm of grape, drove General Bonnet's troops back, step by step, to the Southern and Eastern height. The Royal Fusiliers under Major Beatty, in the front line, carried a height and captured 18 guns.

The failure of the Portuguese to secure the second of the two Arapiles, left the 7th Fusiliers at the mercy of the French Cavalry and Infantry. Lieutenant Cameron who was present thus describes their position, " We were at this moment ordered by Major Beatty to retire and form square, a most hazardous movement when the enemy's Infantry were advancing, and within thirty yards of us. The order was only partially heard and obeyed on the right, while on the left we kept up a hot fire on the enemy, who were advancing up-hill, and within a few yards of us. The companies on our right having retired in succession, we found ourselves alone ; but, the ground the enemy was ascending was so steep, that we got off without loss. Luckily, while we were forming square to receive Cavalry, the 6th

Division came up and received the charge intended for us".

Marmont and General Bonnet were wounded, Thomières was killed, and though General Bertrand Clausel with wonderful ability restored the battle, the repulse in the first forty minutes, after 5 o'clock, was never really re--covered. The fight, however, continued until 10 o'clock, when, under cover of the darkness, Clausel skilfully with--drew, and, from the disordered masses, formed a rear-guard and covered the retreat. The allies lost over 7,000 in killed and wounded ; but, the French loss was not less than 12,000, and 7,000 prisoners and eleven guns. The Royal Fusiliers lost one Officer and 19 men killed, 10 Officers and 170 men wounded.

Thus ended what is considered Wellington's most brilliant battle. The lightning-like stroke when Marmont separated his left from the centre, the screening from the enemy of his own dispositions, his holding back the reserves until the supreme moment, when their appearance seemed to the French to be that of an Army suddenly arising from the ground, are indisputable proofs of good generalship.

This brief outline will help to explain the following letter of Lieutenant Knowles, written three days after the battle, when he was still suffering from the wound in his arm.

To Mr. Robert Knowles.

Salamanca, July 25th, 1812.

Dear Father,—It is with the greatest satisfaction I

write you after the glorious victory of the 22nd instant on the heights of Salamanca. The action commenced about four o'clock, by the enemy driving in our Light Infantry, when our Regt. was ordered to their support, and we drove them back in great style. Immediately a general attack commenced. Our Brigade and a Brigade of Portuguese advanced in line against their centre, the enemy keeping an incessant fire upon us from twelve pieces of artillery, but nothing could check our advance, and the enemy retired from the heights they occupied in the greatest con--fusion. At the same time Genl. Packenham, with the 3rd Division, attacked and turned their left, taking a great number of prisoners, and several pieces of artillery. The enemy again formed upon some heights in front of a large forest, and we commenced a second attack. The enemy, after an obstinate resistance, ran into the woods, great numbers of them throwing away their arms. At the same time the 1st Division turned their right, when the rout became general. Our loss on this memorable day has been very severe :—Genls. Le Marchant and Pack killed, Genls. Beresford, Cotton, Leith, Cole, Clinton, and many other officers of rank wounded. The enemy's loss is estimated at from 10 to 12 thousand men kill'd and wounded, and upwards of four thousand prisoners, with a great number of guns, eagles, and colours. Early in the morning our Army commenced its pursuit, and they have already sent through this town upwards of 4,000 more prisoners. You may calculate upon the destruction of one-half the French Army, as our Army is in full pursuit about 40 miles from this town on the road to Madrid. The French Commissariat have all ran away ; they have no bread or meat, and are killing their horses as a substitute. At the conclusion of the action I received a musquet ball in my left arm, but I had it cut out the same night, and I believe the bone is not injured.

Our Regt., as usual, has suffered considerably, one capt. killed, one captn. wounded, and nine lieuts. Our Brigade does not exceed 500 men, and they are formed into one Battalion. Our loss fell chiefly upon the 3rd, 4th, 5th, and 6th Divisions. The 1st, 7th, and Light Divisions are in high order, and with the Cavalry are strong enough to fight the enemy if they dare to make a stand. I wrote you last from Camp near this town about the 18th ult. We remained in the neighbourhood covering the operations against the Fort at this town. The enemy lay in our front, and some- -times amused us with a brisk cannonade. The 7th Division had a sharp skirmish, driving the enemy from a hill on our right. On the 26th the enemy retired, and the Fort having surrendered, we pursued them. On the 27th the enemy retired upon *Toursde Selas, where they crossed the Douro. We remained in Camp on the opposite side the river near Medina del Campo, until the night of the 15th. On the morning of the 18th the enemy came up with us. A heavy cannonade commenced which lasted the whole day. In the evening they came up with us, and their Infantry attempted to turn our left, but were repulsed with great slaughter by the left Brigade of our Division, sup- -ported by the Portuguese. Another French column advanced, and we advanced to meet them, but they thought proper to retire in double quick time. On the 20th we again retired. On the 21st we had a great deal of manœuv- -ring. On the morning of the 22nd there was a sharp skirmish, which lasted about four hours. Lord Wellington did all in his power to entice them upon a hill immediately in our front, which he at last succeeded in doing, and immediately a general attack commenced. Never did a

---

* Read " Tordesillas." Marmont took the direction of the Douro and moved to Tordesillas—Gleig's Life of Wellington, p. 167.

British Army carry on a campaign with so much success, the surprising Genl. Gerard's Corps in the south, the capture of Ciudad Rodrigo, Badajos, [then] at Almarez, and Salamanca, lastly the destruction of one half the French Army has placed our gallant leader amongst the greatest Generals* of modern Europe, and no recompense his country can make him will be too great. I will write you again by the next post, and give you all the news in my power. Please to remember me to my brothers, sisters, and all enquiring friends, and believe me,

Your affectionate Son,
R. Knowles, Lt., Fusiliers.

P.S.—Excuse all mistakes and bad writing, as my arm is rather painful, and the post is going.

The Royal Fusiliers accompanied Wellington to Madrid and took part in his triumphal entry into the Capital of Spain. It might have been a ceremonial exchange between Governors. At 6 o'clock in the morning of the 12th August, King Joseph with his court left, and at noon Wellington with his Army marched into Madrid.

Lieutenant Knowles made light of his wound in his home-letters ; but, it was officially described as "severe", and, as he was suffering in addition from fever and ague, he was remaining at Salamanca. The evidence of this is circumstantially precise. It is, moreover, certain that his

---

* Note.—In the " Bible in Spain ", by George Borrow, the Spanish curé says that Wellington and General Craufurd dined in his house after the battle. Wellington may have dined there, but Craufurd was lying on the ramparts of Ciudad Rodrigo.

next letter, bearing the post mark " Lisbon, September 23rd, 1812," was written at Salamanca.

Postmark, " Lisbon. Se. 23, 1812 ".

To Mr. Robert Knowles.

Dear Father,—I have been under the necessity of breaking my promise in my letter of the 25th ult., which was to write to you by the next post. I hope you have received it long before this, as it would satisfy you that my wound was of a trifling nature, and I am happy to say that it is now completely healed. Immediately after closing my last letter to you, I was attacked by the ague fever and a most severe bowel complaint, with which I have ever since been confined to my bed, with the exception of four or five days. I trust that I have now banished all my complaints, as I have not had a fit of the ague this last three days, and I am rapidly recovering my strength. I yesterday rode as far as the field of battle, but found myself so very weak that I could not ride over the ground. Our wounded in this town are rapidly recovering, but the officers are extremely ill off, not having a farthing to purchase the comforts which are necessary to men nearly reduced to skeletons by wounds and sickness. The Army is only paid up to the 24th March, but they had the generosity to give to each wounded officer 20 dollars a few days after our arrival in this town. This sum (to a few who nursed it well) has supply'd the necessarys of life ; others have sold their horses, asses, or mules ; others their epaulettes, watches, rings, etc., and, to the disgrace of John Bull, others have perished for want. These are the sufferings which British wounded officers have been subject to in this town, but thanks to Providence I have not been subject to the least inconvenience. Fortunately I had a few dollars in my possession when I came into the town, which have enabled me to get nearly all a person in my sickly situation could desire. You cannot expect news from me now that I am so far in the rear. The last accounts from the Army they were still in quarters ; the 1st, 4th, 5th, and 7th Divns. at the Escurial, the 3rd and Light Divns. at Madrid, the 6th Divn., with the 4th, 5th, 38th, 42nd, and 82nd Regts. were watching the remains of Marmont's Army. Report says that General Maitland has landed at Alicant with an expedition from Sicily. We are anxious to hear what the Russians are doing. I hope they will keep the enemy employed in the north until this country is cleared of them. The Spaniards seem to be actively employed recruiting. The general outcry amongst them is " Let us have British officers and we will fight like British soldiers ". It is now about thirteen months since I left England, and I have in that time only received three letters from home, the last dated 29th Feby. It is natural to conclude that they could not always miscarry, and therefore that no one writes to me. The subject of Lt. Devey, which I have often wrote about, has given me a great deal of uneasiness. Whether you have lodged the £20 I have so repeatedly mentioned in his hands I am ignorant of. He is now returned to England on account of a wound and bad health. The last communication I had with him he proposed that I should give him your address, and he would write to you for the sum of ten pounds which I have received from him. On his arrival in England, therefore, if you have not lodged the money, I beg you will remit him the sum of ten pounds the first intimation you receive from him, and I also beg that you will pay the postage of all letters to him. I have before stated to you that the Army was six months in arrear of pay, which must be sufficient to show you at once my situation. I have lately been under the necessity of purchasing clothing, etc., to a considerable amount. I am therefore under the most disagreeable but pressing necessity of begging a further remittance of £25, which I request you will lodge in my name in the hands of Messrs. Greenwood and Co., Army Agents, and desire them to write to me on the receipt of it. By the same post you lodge the money I hope you will write me an account of it. It is extremely painful for me to ask this last remittance ; nothing but real want should oblige me to do it. I hope my health will shortly be re-established (it has been very precarious since the seige of Badajos). If it is not, I shall be under the necessity of effecting an exchange into a regt. serving in some other climate. Give my best respects to Mr. Lomax's family, and to all enquiring friends ; remember me to my brothers and sisters, and believe me,

Your affectionate Son,

R. Knowles, Lt. Fusiliers.

P.S.—As I do not receive letters from home, it may probably be owing to this circumstance that the postage of all letters for abroad must be paid in England, otherwise they will not be sent.

The condition of the wounded who were left at Salamanca was deplorable, and it remains a disgraceful reproach to the British Government of the day. They were without the actual necessities of life, many of them were in want of food, clothing, and medicines. The Army was in arrears of pay, and the Commander-in-chief had not the means for paying the butcher's bill. Many more of the

sick and wounded would have died, but for the Commissary-
-General, Sir James McGrigor, who sent stores from Madrid
on his own responsibility, without authority, and he was
censured for so doing.

It is obvious that Lieutenant Knowles, on account of
his wound and disease, was unequal for some months to
march with his regiment, and to endure the hardships of
the campaign. This explains his presence at the Depôt
which was established at Santarem on the Tagus, about
fifty miles from Lisbon. There is now a gap in the corres-
-pondence ; for, there is no letter between September 23rd,
1812 and February 7th, 1813, the last of the series, and
this is much to be regretted. We can, however, imagine
the spectacle of a high-spirited young officer, rejoicing in
restoration to health, and chafing at the inaction of an
enforced detention at a Depôt, when his regiment is in the
field. A staff-appointment, with its daily increase of five
shillings to a subaltern's pay, does not lessen his zeal to
be with his comrades in the fighting-line, and, in June, he
is again with his regiment.

To Mr. Robert Knowles.

Santarem, Feby. 7th, 1813.

Dear Father,—I wrote you last from Lisbon on the
19th Dec., and returned to this on the 24th same month.
I was so far recovered that I immediately applied for

permission to join my Regt., but was unfortunately detained to do duty in this Depot. About three weeks ago I was ordered to act as Adjutant, and I am still pestered with that troublesome office. From nine o'clock in the morning till six in the evening I have not a spare minute. The con--stant employment I have had, and the uncertainty of remaining here, has been the cause of my delaying writing to you much longer than I intended. With my new office, I have become a man of business ; every post-day I have eight or more letters to answer, and weekly we send in about fifty returns to Hd. Quarters. The Commandant, in direct opposition to my wishes, has reported me to the Adjt. Genl. as a stationary officer at this Depot, so that I can see no prospect of leaving for some time. The last letter I received from home was dated the 17th Nov. The late severe family losses you have sustained distress me excessively, but the miseries I have witnessed and partially endured in this country have in some measure hardened my feelings. It is a subject I cannot dwell upon, therefore will close it. The last mail brought us the most glorious news from Russia ; it appears to be almost incredible the success they have obtained over the common enemy. I now feel confident that the business in this country will be decided the ensuing summer, and that I shall soon have the satisfac--tion of returning to my native land, and conversing about my adventures in the Peninsula.

We have no news at this Depot, therefore must conclude. Remember me to my brothers, sisters, and all enquiring friends, and believe me to remain,

Your affectionate Son,

R. Knowles.

Feby. 9th, 1813.

Our Lt.-Col. Blakeney* passed through this town this morning on his march to the Army. I mentioned my being detained here, and my having been applied to for to accept the Adjutancy of this Depot. He strongly recommended me to join my Regt., but finding that I should not be allowed to do so at present, he advised me to accept the situation of Adjt., saying that, if I must be absent from my regiment, he saw no reason that I should not receive 5s. per day extra, so long as I should be detained. Until I write you the contrary, be so kind as to direct to me at Santarem.

In February, 1813, the Royal Fusiliers were at Castle Melhor, on the right bank of the Coa, and, towards the end of May, they crossed the Douro and marched to Salamanca. There is no record of the date when Lieutenant Knowles

---

* Note.—Lieut.-Col. Blakeney became Field-Marshal the Right Honourable Sir Edward Blakeney, G.C.B., G.C.H. He joined the Royal Fusiliers as Major on the 24th March, 1804, and he was promoted Brevet Lieutenant-Colonel in 1808, and Colonel in 1811. He served with distinction at the capture of Demerara, Berbice, and Essequibo in 1796, and in these operations he had the exceptional experience of being three times taken prisoner by privateers. In 1799, he fought at Egmont-op-Zee and Krabbendem in Holland. He accom--panied the expedition to Copenhagen in 1807, and, in 1810, he was again in the West Indies at the capture of Martinique. In that year he went to the Peninsula in command of the 1st Battalion of the Royal Fusiliers, and he was at the head of it in the hard fought battles of Busaco and Albuera, the affair at Aldea da Ponte, the Sieges of Ciudad Rodrigo and Badajoz, the battles of Vittoria, Pyrenees and Nivelle, as well as in various minor actions. He went with the Fusiliers to New Orleans, where he was present at the unfortunate attack on the American lines when General Pakenham was killed. In the Peninsula, he was twice wounded. He served with the Army of occupation in Paris in 1815. He died on the 2nd August, 1868, when he was the Senior Field-Marshal in the Army, and when he had been Governor of the Chelsea Hospital for 12 years.

was released from the duties of Adjutant of the Depôt, or when he rejoined his regiment ; but, it was most probably during May. From May 25th to June 19th, Wellington pursued the French, whose rearguard he caught on the left bank of the Bayas. With the Light Division he turned the enemy's left flank, attacking them at the same time in front with the 4th Division. The Fusilier Brigade now consisted of the 7th and 23rd Fusiliers, and the 20th and 48th regiments, under Major--General Robert Ross. They all participated in the attack made by the 4th Division. The 7th surprised the French in the village of Montevite, and, with the 20th, followed in pursuit, driving them across the river Zadora. The Fusilier Brigade on the following day held a position on the banks of the Bayas, while the Army was concen--trating for a general attack. King Joseph Bonaparte had taken up a position six miles in length and in front of Vittoria, which stands on some rising ground. Wellington's plan of battle was to assail both flanks and, when they had been turned, to send three Divisions against their front. The flank attacks were successful, and the frontal attack was set in motion, when with impetuosity the 3rd Division under Picton broke right through the French centre. With his centre broken and both flanks crushed in, King Joseph had no alternative but to retreat. The last stand was made on some low hills where the fire of eighty guns checked Picton's victorious advance : but, the 4th

Division rushing onwards stormed one hill and forced the French to retire from the others. The Royal Fusiliers took up a position at the bridge of Nanclares. The retreat of the French now became a running-fight for six miles, and, in the confusion and haste, they abandoned guns, baggage, and treasure to the value of one million sterling. There were in some Divisions of the Army excesses ; but, in spite of the temptation of rich spoils of war, the discipline of the Royal Fusiliers was such that they marched on, not a man leaving the ranks. On short rations for six weeks, and without food on the 21st, the day of the battle, the men were half starving, and, when they halted at 9 o'clock, they feasted with unbridled indulgence on the sheep, wine and biscuits, which the French had left behind them. The pursuit of the enemy was continued on the 22nd. After a long march, the 7th encamped in the neighbourhood of Pampeluna. On July 18th, the 4th Division marched to the Pyrenees and took up a position in the valley of Urroz, the 7th being two miles in advance at Espinal. On the 24th, they were posted on a mountain to the West of Roncesvalles, in order to secure the pass. Marshal Soult, by whom King Joseph Bonaparte had been superseded, finding the allies were holding a long scattered line, boldly determined to drive them from the Pyrenees. On the morning of July 25th, he fiercely attacked General Byng's Brigade of the 2nd Division at Roncesvalles. While this combat was proceeding, the Fusilier Brigade advanced

F

under General Ross, up the Mandechari pass, and at
Lindouz they came suddenly upon the head of General
Reille's column, which was pushing forward to secure the
pass of Atalosti, and thus to cut off Campbell's Portuguese
Brigade. Ross could act only on a very narrow front, yet
he sent his foremost companies against the French column.
This vigorous action secured the pass, and gave General
Cole time to concentrate his forces : but, the pass was
secured with the loss of many brave soldiers and, among
them, was Lieutenant Robert Knowles, the only Officer
of the 7th Fusiliers who fell on that day. Thus ended,
in his twenty-fourth year, the career of this young
Englishman. The space of his active military life was two
years, but within that short period he had taken part in the
two sieges of Ciudad Rodrigo and Badajoz, the action at
Aldea da Ponte, and the battles of Salamanca and Vittoria.
He suffered bodily-sickness from privations and hardships,
and he was wounded twice. At Roncesvalles, he won a
soldier's death. There are two qualities which especially
appear in the letters, namely, family-affection and the
bravery of the soldier. In Japan he would be an ancestor
whose spirit would be the object of worship. His life was
a fulfilment of the family motto : *nec diu nec frustra*—not
for long, and not in vain. His contemporaries, friends,
and neighbours, showed their appreciation of his character
and services by erecting to his memory a monument which
bears the following inscription :—

Inscription on a Monument in the Parish Church of St. Peter, Bolton-le-Moors, Lancashire.

Nec diu nec frustra.

To the Memory of Lieutenant Robert Knowles, a Native of this Parish, who volunteered May 6th, 1811, from the 1st Royal Lancashire Militia into the 7th Regiment of Fusiliers, then united with the British Army in the expul- -sion of the French from Spain. He distinguished himself at the taking of Ciudad Rodrigo and at Badajos, where he commanded part of a detachment appointed to storm Fort St. Roque. Such was his intrepidity, that having first mounted the wall and succeeded in his enterprise, he opened the Gates to the remainder of the detachment and received the command of the Fort. He behaved with much courage at Salamanca and Vittoria, at the former of which places he was severely wounded. This brave young man fell in the hard-contested Action at the Pass of Ronces- -valles, in the Pyrenees, July 25th, 1813, in the 24th year of his age.

This Monument is erected as a just tribute to so much heroism and worth by his Fellow Townsmen, A.D. 1816.

THE KNOWLES FAMILY.

The Knowles family have been long established in Bolton. In the pedigree which appears in Baines's History of the County Palatine and Duchy of Lancaster, edited by James Croston, F.S.A., vol. 3, page 222, their descent is traced from John Knowle or Knowles, of Edgworth, the son of Richard Knowle or Knowles, who died about the year 1582, and was buried at Bolton. Hereunder is a portion of the pedigree in which occur the names intro- -duced in the correspondence, together with some later names of members of the family. A very striking feature is the succession of ten members of the Knowles family down to the present day with the alternate names of Robert and Andrew—a long succession, which the Heralds' College think particularly interesting and perhaps unique. A Court Roll of 1651 relating to the Manor of Tottington, a township contiguous to Quarlton, proves that the Robert Knowles who lived at Quarlton Old Hall, commonly known as Top o' Quarlton, and died in 1701, was of sufficient age to succeed his grandfather, Richard, as heir to the Hawkshaw Estate, which has des- -cended to the Robert Knowles, of Ednaston Lodge, Derby.

See "Genealogy of the Knowles Family of Edgworth, Quarlton, Quarlton, Little Bolton, and Swinton," by the late James C. Scholes, reprinted for private circulation from the "Bolton Journal" of January 23rd, 1886.

ROBERT KNOWLES. Buried at Turton, 1701.
Of Quarlton.
|
ANDREW KNOWLES. Buried at Turton, 1730.
Of Quarlton.
|
ROBERT KNOWLES. Buried at Turton, 1780.
Of Little Bolton.
|
ANDREW KNOWLES. Buried at Turton, 1810.
Of Quarlton and Eagley Bank, Little Bolton.
|
ROBERT KNOWLES. Buried at Turton, 1819.
Of Eagley Bank.

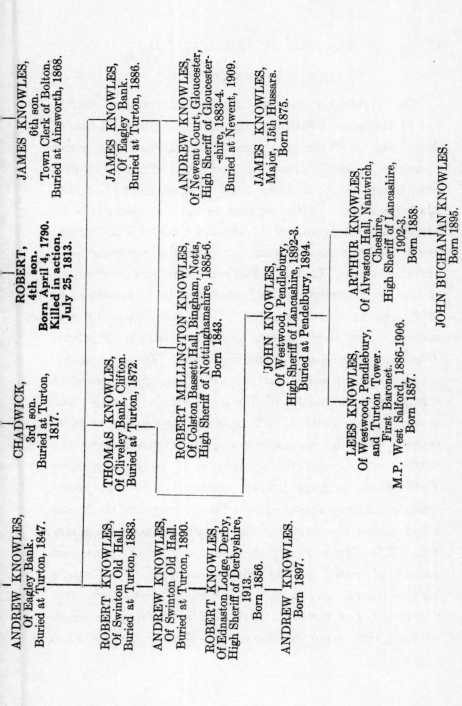

CHADWICK,
3rd son.
Buried at Turton,
1817.

ROBERT,
4th son.
Born April 4, 1790.
Killed in action,
July 25, 1813.

JAMES KNOWLES,
6th son.
Town Clerk of Bolton.
Buried at Ainsworth, 1868.

ANDREW KNOWLES,
Of Eagley Bank.
Buried at Turton, 1847.

THOMAS KNOWLES,
Of Cliveley Bank, Clifton.
Buried at Turton, 1872.

JAMES KNOWLES,
Of Eagley Bank.
Buried at Turton, 1886.

ROBERT KNOWLES,
Of Swinton Old Hall.
Buried at Turton, 1883.

ANDREW KNOWLES,
Of Swinton Old Hall.
Buried at Turton, 1890.

ROBERT MILLINGTON KNOWLES,
Of Colston Bassett Hall, Bingham, Notts,
High Sheriff of Nottinghamshire, 1885-6.
Born 1843.

ANDREW KNOWLES,
Of Newent Court, Gloucester,
High Sheriff of Gloucester-
-shire, 1883-4.
Buried at Newent, 1909.

ROBERT KNOWLES,
Of Ednaston Lodge, Derby,
High Sheriff of Derbyshire,
1913.
Born 1856.

JAMES KNOWLES,
Major, 15th Hussars.
Born 1875.

ANDREW KNOWLES.
Born 1897.

JOHN KNOWLES,
Of Westwood, Pendlebury,
High Sheriff of Lancashire, 1892-3.
Buried at Pendelbury, 1894.

LEES KNOWLES,
Of Westwood, Pendlebury,
and Turton Tower.
First Baronet.
M.P. West Salford, 1886-1906.
Born 1857.

ARTHUR KNOWLES,
Of Alvaston Hall, Nantwich,
Cheshire,
High Sheriff of Lancashire,
1902-3.
Born 1858.

JOHN BUCHANAN KNOWLES.
Born 1895.

GENERAL PAKENHAM.

The Honorable Edward Michael Pakenham, second
son of the second Baron Longford and brother-in-law of
the Duke of Wellington, who had married his sister
Catherine in 1806, joined the Army in 1792, and his first
commission seems to have been that of Captain in the
92nd Regiment. After serving in several Regiments as
Major, he was promoted Lieutenant-Colonel in 1799, and
five years later he was transferred to the command of a
battalion of the 7th Royal Fusiliers. He was at the head
of the 1st Battalion in the expedition to Copenhagen in
1807, and at the capture of Martinique, where he was
wounded. In 1809 he was appointed Deputy-Adjutant-
-General to the Army in the Peninsula. There he subse-
-quently served with marked distinction in command of
a Brigade at the battles of Busaco, Fuentes de Oñoro, and
in many minor actions. His crowning service was at Sala-
-manca where he commanded the 3rd Division, began the
battle, and successfully brought to a triumphant issue
Wellington's brilliant stroke. General Pakenham com-
-manded the expedition against New Orleans, where he was
killed during the attack on the American lines on January
8th, 1815. Thus died Pakenham " the most frank and
gallant of men", in the thirty-sixth year of his age, a
Major-General and a G.C.B. General Pakenham died
unmarried, but the elder branch of his family, the Earls
of Longford, have continued the line of distinguished

soldiers.   His younger brother, Lieutenant-General Sir Hercules R. Pakenham, served with distinction : his eldest son was killed at the battle of Inkerman, and his third son, Lieutenant-General Thomas Henry Pakenham, C.B., of Longford Lodge, County Antrim, Colonel of the East Lancashire Regiment, died February 21st, 1913, aged 86 years. Lieutenant-General Thomas Henry Pakenham, therefore, was a nephew of Major-General Sir Edward Michael Pakenham, who, acting on the command of Wellington, gave the word to his Division and began the movement which won the battle of Salamanca.   He en--tered the Army in 1844, and served in the Crimea, being present at the battle of the Alma, in which he was twice wounded. His eldest son is Colonel Hercules Arthur Pakenham, commanding the London Irish.

THE DUKE OF WELLINGTON.

Mr. James Knowles, the brother of Lieutenant Robert Knowles, sent the letter of July 25th, 1812, describing the battle of Salamanca, written as it was by one who had fought there, to the Duke of Wellington, and in reply he received the following characteristic note. These notes were not uncommon, and they were always in the hand-writing of the Duke, who replied, as a rule, without the delay of a day :—

London, May 21st, 1849.

James Knowles, Esq.,
    Bolton.

F.M. the Duke of Wellington presents his compliments to Mr. Knowles.

The Duke thanks Mr. Knowles for sending him the letter from his brother written at Salamanca on the 25th July, 1812, giving an account of the Battle of Salamanca, in which he had been present.

He has read the letter with much interest, and returns it.

EXTRACT FROM COLBURN'S UNITED SERVICE MAGAZINE,
December, 1872.

" For a few days the Fusiliers were employed in the blockade of Pampeluna, until the 25th, when they formed part of the force detached to Logrono to intercept General Clausel, who was there with a Division of French who had joined in the battle. Clausel, however, by what Wellington describes as ' some extraordinary forced marches', escaped. The Fusiliers returned to the vicinity of Pampeluna, where they remained a few days, proceeding subsequently to the Pyrenees, the first Division taking post at Viscayret, in the valley of Urroz, the Royal Fusiliers being at Espinal, two miles in advance. On the 2nd July, Soult collected the right and left wings of his army, and on the 25th attacked General Bying's post at Roncesvalles. Lieutenant-General Cole moved up to his support with the First Division. Two companies of the Royal Fusiliers had been advanced on the 24th July to a height westward of Roncesvalles, where they were joined by the remainder of the Battalion during the night, and were consequently ready to meet the French attack. Some sharp fighting occurred during the day, in which the Royal Fusiliers lost Lieutenant Knowles, and six men, killed ; one sergeant and 23 men, wounded."

ADDENDUM.

A Letter from the above-mentioned Andrew Orrell.

Andrew Orrell served with his friend Robert Knowles in the Peninsula. He was Ensign in the 34th Regiment, and a letter of this light-hearted soldier speaks for itself :—

Appes.   Oct. 4th, 1812.

Yours of the 22nd I received on our march at Quintana. Not having time to answer it before, I now take the oppor--tunity, as we have halted two days. How much longer we shall remain, I cannot say ; but, as we are but eight leagues from Madrid, a great party of the officers are gone to visit that city ; but, for my part, I shall wait a chance of the Brigade going that way, as our marches have been very considerable. We cross'd the Tagus at Almaraz and marched on for Talavera and Toledo ; by the map, you will be able to see our route, as we went by Zafra and Altons and turned to our left, expecting Soult to have gone through La Mancha for Madrid. But the Ape has com--pletely dropt our acquaintance and gone for Valentia with sixty thousand men, and report says that he left that place too ; if so, he must have seen his own shadow, as there is no troops to do him much harm : he seems very dis--content about things. The people seem all alive here, and strive who can make the most amusement. Last night there was a splendid ball given us, and they requested Brigadier Wilson to give it in orders that they expected all officers to attend ; there was a very good turn out of females. We have crost as fine a country as ever was seen, and the town of Toledo is beyond anything I expected to have found ; its magnificence is fitting only to be described on a winter's night, when time is not measured. We have abundance of everything, except money : as we have not been paid since April, it is become a scarce thing, but the Spanish Sutlers that accompany the Army, having great confidence in British Officers, supply us on credit with anything we want as teas, sugars, etc. As to pretend to give any particulars as to military affairs is out of the question, but that the French seem to shun us as much as they can. Some people think the game is up, but I think there will be one great struggle. Our confidence is great, and well it may, for our troops are fat, ragged, and saucy ; but, never mind ! Clothing is coming after us from Lisbon. Wine is abundant in this place, and the inhabitants being free with it, the great difficulty is to keep the men sober. What we shall do next I cannot say, so we must leave it for time to determine. Let me hear from you when this arrives, and often. You mention Mr. Bentley, Captain G. Bambers, etc. When you see them, remember me to them, likewise to Andrew Knowles,* and any of the family you may converse with. I hope my Sisters and Brother John are well. . . . I shall conclude with wishing you all every happiness. Remember me to my Uncle and Aunt, etc., etc. W. Bradshaw never wrote to me.—Yours,

A. Orrell,

Ensn. 34th Regt.,

2nd Division British Army, Spain.

(Endorsed) Recd. Novr. 6th, 1812.

---

* The eldest brother of Lieut. Robert Knowles, Andrew Knowles, of Eagley Bank, Bolton, was born April 16th, 1783, and died December 8th, 1847 ; buried at Turton ; will proved at Chester, May 27th, 1848.

A description from a manuscript endorsement of the service in the Army of Lieutenant Andrew Orrell, who was the younger son of the first Orrell of Meadowcroft Farm, Quarlton.

1803— Sept. 15th.	The service of Lieut. Andrew Orrell, of the 34 Regiment. Then entered Volunteer in the Bolton Volunteer Corps under Lieut.-Colonel Fletcher, being then under 18 years of age, and recd. a Commission for a Lieut. in the Local Militia. Then in the Royal Lancashire Militia.
1811— July 16th Left Lancashire for the Army.	Then Volunteer'd to the Line and went to Spain. Was in several skirmishes, was at the affair of Ria de Malina (*sic*), and got a slight wound in his right hand.
Left Lancashire for the Army.	Was at the Battle of Ronces Valles (*sic*), where he got a severe wound : a ball entered his left breast, and came out within an inch and half of his spine. Remained with the Army till the re--duction (Line), and went to Spain.

Lieutenant Andrew Orrell was with Lieutenant Knowles in General Hill's Division. He retired on half-pay at the conclusion of the war, lived at Greenthorne, Edgworth, as Colonel Andrew Orrell, and, dying in 1853, he was buried in Turton Churchyard. One of his daughters, Miss Elizabeth Ann Orrell, now resides at 65, Wellington Road, Turton. It may be of interest to mention that Turton Tower was early in the 15th century, and until 1628, in the possession of the Orrell family, and that now it has passed to the Knowles family.

A COMMISSION OF 1809.

The Right Honorable Edward Earl of Derby, Lord Lieutenant of the County Palatine of Lancaster, **To** Andrew Orrell, Gentleman.

By Virtue of His Majesty's Commission under His Great Seal of Great Britain constituting me His Lieutenant in and for the County Palatine of Lancaster and in pursuance of the several Statutes in that case made and provided and of the Authorities and powers thereby given and of all other powers and Authorities enabling me there-unto I have presented to His Majesty and **have** (by and with His Approbation) constituted appointed and given Commission And by these Presents **Do** constitute appoint and give Commission to you the said Andrew Orrell to be an Ensign in the First Battalion of the Royal Lancashire Militia forces raised and to be raised for and within the said County Palatine whereof Thomas Stanley Esquire is Colonel pursuant to the said Acts And you are hereby required to train and discipline the persons to be armed and arrayed by Virtue of the several Statutes relating to the Militia forces and in all Things to conform yourself to the Duty of an Ensign of the Militia forces according to the Rules Orders and Directions of the several Acts of Parlia-ment relating thereto and to the true Intent and Meaning thereof. **Given** under my Hand and Seal this thirty-first Day of July in the forty-ninth year of the Reign of our Sovereign Lord George the third and in the year of our Lord one thousand eight hundred and nine.

(Signed) DERBY.   (L. S.)

A CENTENARY.

Fermoy,
Co. Cork,
July 1st, 1913.

Dear Sir Lees Knowles,—In the name of the 1st Battalion Royal Fusiliers, I beg to thank you most sincerely for your kindness in proposing to dedicate a room in the Union Jack Club for the use of the Royal Fusiliers in memory of your great-great-Uncle. I am sure that this tribute to a gallant Fusilier will be warmly appreciated by all ranks now serving in the Regiment. . . . . .

I remain,
Yours very truly,
(Signed) R. Fowler-Butler,
Lt.-Col.
Comdg. 1st Batt^n Royal Fusiliers.

———◆———

UNION JACK CLUB,
91a, Waterloo Road, London, S.E.

———

Room N° 351.

———

To the Royal Fusiliers,
in Memory of
Lieutenant Robert Knowles,
who fell at Roncesvalles,
July 25th, 1813,
dedicated by his relative,
Sir Lees Knowles, Bar^t, C.V.O.,
July 25th, 1913.

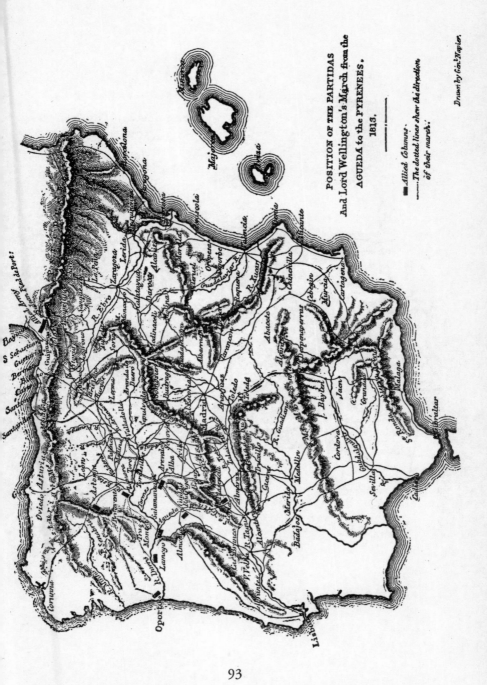

POSITION OF THE PARTIDAS
And Lord Wellington's March from the
AGUEDA to the PYRENEES.
1813.

■ Allied Columns.
⋯⋯ The dotted lines shew the direction
of their march.

Drawn by Col. Napier.

Soults operations to relieve
PAMPELUNA
July 1813.

94

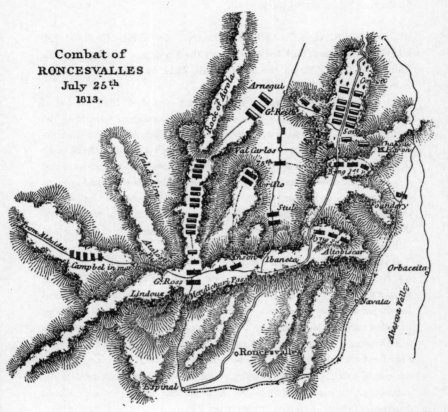

Combat of
RONCESVALLES
July 25th
1813.

Rock of Airola

Arnegui

Gl Reite

Sou

Val Carlos

25th

hapel
K Baron

Morillo

Byng 1st

Stule

Foundry

from Althides

Byng 2

Altobiscar

Campbel in march

Atequiste

Sanson

Ibaneta

Orbaceita

Gl Ross

Merdichuri Pass

Navala

Lindoux

Aldescoa Valley

Espinal

Roncesvalles

Valde Airo

Drawn by Genl Napier.

95

Also published in facsimile in *The Spellmount Library of Military History* and available from all good bookshops. In case of difficulty, please contact Spellmount Publishers (01580 893730).

RECOLLECTIONS OF THE STORMING OF THE CASTLE OF BADAJOZ: by the Third Division, under the Command of Lieut Gen Sir Thomas Picton GCB, on the 6th of April, 1812 by Captain MacCarthy
Introduction by Ian Fletcher

The siege and storming of Badajoz, from 18 March to 6 April 1812, was one of the bloodiest episodes of the Peninsular War. In conditions resembling the trenches of the First World War, Wellington's infantry dug their way towards the huge medieval walls of the Spanish frontier fortress before storming the place on the night of 6 April. The town had denied them on two previous occasions and it is little wonder that once inside the men went beserk and embarked upon an orgy of rape, pillage and destruction that lasted for a full seventy-two hours. Even the iron hand of Wellington himself could not stop it, and, in the words of one of the great historians of the war, "the disorder subsided, rather than it was quelled."

The storming of Badajoz was not achieved without huge cost to Wellington, however. Indeed, he watched, helpless, as the flower of his army was smashed upon the breaches. Over forty times did the 4th and Light Divisions attack, and forty times were they beaten back with heavy loss. Fortunately, two other attacks, intended only to distract the French succeeded. One of them was made by the 3rd Division, who took the Castle of Badajoz by escalade, the men scaling the forty feet high walls by means of flimsy ladders. The 3rd Division was guided to its point of attack by James MacCarthy, whose own vivid account of the siege and storming is reproduced here in this facsimile, the latest in the acclaimed *Spellmount Library of Military History* series.

As well as being a graphic account of the siege, MacCarthy's book is both extremely rare and is much sought after by students of the Peninsular War and by book collectors alike.

THE PRIVATE JOURNAL OF JUDGE-ADVOCATE LARPENT: attached to the Headquarters of Lord Wellington during the Peninsular War, from 1812 to its close by Francis Seymour Larpent
Introduction by Ian C Robertson
Originally published in 1853, this is a facsimile of the third edition of one of the five contemporary journals, later published without alteration, which Sir Charles Oman has referred to as being an interesting and not always discreet account of his busy life at Head-Quarters, and among the best for hard facts.
In September 1812, the 36 years old Frances Larpent set sail for Lisbon to take up the exacting position of Judge-Advocate-General with the responsibility of reforming and simplifying the disciplinary machinery of courts-martial throughout Wellington's army in the Peninsula, where no form of professional regulation had yet been instituted.
In almost daily contact with Wellington, Larpent's narrative is of especial interest as being written from the point of view of a non-combatant.
This volume is a "must" for all students of the Peninsular War in general and the Duke of Wellington in particular.

MILITARY MEMOIRS OF FOUR BROTHERS: engaged in the service of their country as well as in The New World and Africa, as on the Continent of Europe by The Survivor (Thomas Fernyhough)
Introduction by Philip Haythornthwaite
Military Memoirs of Four Brothers, first published in 1829 and reprinted for the first time, in the Spellmount Library of Military History, since 1838, is an extremely rare record of the military service of one family during the Napoleonic Wars.
The Fernyhoughs of Lichfield provided four officers to the British naval and military forces, two of whom died on service with the Royal Marines. The letters and journals of two of the brothers provide a fascinating account of some of the more important, and some of the lesser-known campaigns and operations of the period, including the Trafalgar campaign, the expedition to South America, and the Peninsular War, Robert Fernyhough serving in the latter with that most elite and famous corps, the 95th Rifles, later the Rifle Brigade.
Thomas Fernyhough, the brother who compiled the account, was a noted historian and researcher, and produced a book which is not only one of the rarest contemporary memoirs of the Napoleonic Wars, but one which illuminates the services and tribulations of a typical military family at this most crucial period in British history.

For a free catalogue, telephone

Spellmount Publishers on

01580 893730

or write to

The Village Centre

Staplehurst

Kent TN12 0BJ

United Kingdom

(Facsimile 01580 893731)

(e-mail enquiries@spellmount.com)

(Website www.spellmount.com)